Building Better Brands

Honk
if you love
Maker's.
Maker's Mark
KENTUCKY STRAIGHT BOURBON
WHISKY
BILLY ELLIOT
THE MUSICAL
BEST PLAY
AUGUST
HEIGHTS
BEST MUSICAL
Coca-Cola
AMERICAN EAGLE OUTFITTERS

Building Better Brands

A Comprehensive Guide to Brand Strategy and Identity Development

SCOTT LERMAN

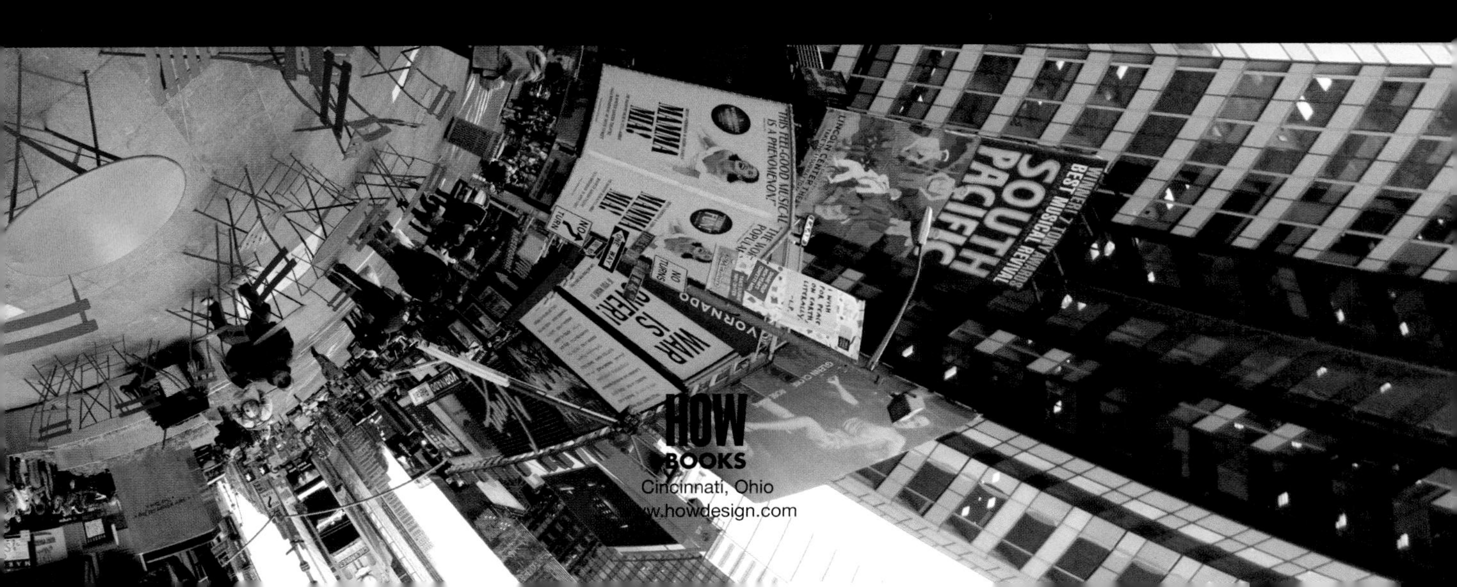

HOW BOOKS
Cincinnati, Ohio
ww.howdesign.com

 Published by HOW Books, an imprint of F+W Media, Inc., 10151 Carver Road, Suite 200, Blue Ash, Ohio 45242. (800) 289-0963. First edition.

For more excellent books and resources for designers, visit www.howdesign.com.

17 16 15 14 13 5 4 3 2 1

ISBN-13: 978-1-4403-3143-5

Distributed in Canada by Fraser Direct
100 Armstrong Avenue
Georgetown, Ontario, Canada L7G 5S4
Tel: (905) 877-4411

Distributed in the U.K. and Europe by F&W Media International, LTD
Brunel House, Forde Close, Newton Abbot, TQ12 4PU, UK
Tel: (+44) 1626 323200, Fax: (+44) 1626 323319
Email: enquiries@fwmedia.com

Distributed in Australia by Capricorn Link
P.O. Box 704, Windsor, NSW 2756 Australia
Tel: (02) 4560-1600

Illustrations by Will Ayres

Dedication

To Susan.

Who is the brand champion? The defender of brand equity and force for competitive change? Who can rally an entire organization to live the full promise of a brand? You.

Given the right knowledge, tools, and help you can ensure a bright future for your brand. Just read on.

Contents

RANDOM
ACTS
OF
BRAND
ING

Introduction

Every organization, every brand, must grow. While some are defined at birth by a single product or service most companies quickly grow not just in scale, but in complexity. And that complexity extends far beyond products, services, and geographic markets. Over time, the established culture of an organization is challenged by mergers and acquisitions, changing leadership, and social forces, raising fundamental issues of "who we are" and "how we will act."

These are the forces of brand entropy, the decay of order into chaos—a descent into random acts of branding. As companies grow, their employees, leaders, and divisions develop their own distinct view of the core purpose and character of the organization and its brand. The result is inefficiency, openings that can be exploited by competitors, and a fundamental misalignment of organizational efforts. Even the best—especially the best—companies begin to unravel a bit as they evolve. It's a natural outgrowth of growth.

So how do you guide the evolution of a brand in a way that returns to the clarity and focus of its founding, while leveraging hard-won scale and diversity? It can be daunting. You must reconcile traditions with aspirations. Shed baggage. Adapt to acquisitions, changing markets, shifting demographics, and more. Win over skeptics and overpower heel-draggers. The benefits (and perils) of redefining a corporate brand are high. You've got to get it right the first time.

"We were a not-for-profit doing great things, but with little appreciation or expertise for developing and managing our brand. We changed all of that."

—Carmenchu Mendiola-Fernández was a mid-level staffer when she led the redefinition of The Washington Center brand.

"NCNB was a Southerner with big ambitions—NationsBank-sized ambitions! Seven years later we acquired (and re-branded) Bank of America."

—Van Perry was a real estate VP at NCNB when he led a team to create the first truly national bank brand.

"A third of DuPont was being spun-off. It was a time when you either became an agent- or victim-of-change. We chose to step up with Steve McCracken and change everything."

—Carol Gee was global brand manager of the DuPont brand when she stepped-up to lead the rebranding of DuPont's synthetic fibers businesses as INVISTA.

You may imagine that only a CEO can refocus an organization and its brand, but that hasn't been my experience. While senior leaders often spark (and must ultimately endorse) change, brand redefinition is almost always led by a loyal, perceptive, and persistent person from the rank and file. Efforts must deeply engage senior management, but the real force of change comes from the heart of the organization.

I've worked with small, medium, and global companies to define their brands and led several of the industry's leading branding firms. But this book is not a recounting of tales from the executive suite or the trenches. It does not extol the brilliance of brands like Apple. It is not a celebration of my greatest branding triumphs.

This book distills what I've learned from decades in the business into understandable and actionable frameworks for developing and redefining a brand. It includes many of the lessons that I teach at the Masters branding program that I helped found at SVA. It is a practical step-by-step guide for how to change everything. Let me know what you accomplish!

Scott Lerman

Building Better Brands?

Too much of brand development is clouded in mystery and obscured by jargon. While "I'll know it when I see it" isn't a sufficient standard, you don't need to be a high-powered consultant to evaluate the effectiveness of a brand.

The answer to "What does it take to build a better brand?" won't be found in brand valuation studies. Arguably, their fundamental analytics aren't much more reliable than "most sexy man" rankings, but that's not the issue. Even a perfect brand valuation methodology would measure an economic symptom, not a cause.

So how can you determine if a brand is effective? What is the right measure for whether a brand, your brand, could be better? Consider three essential elements.

A great brand is actionable, compelling, and true. Two out of three won't do. It must be a blend of all three.

Actionable. When a brand idea is actionable, everyone responsible for what is made, said, and done knows the do's and don'ts for success.

Actionable brands are simply the "root of all… actions." They provide an unambiguous standard for behavior. They set a benchmark for products and services. They set the pitch and tenor of the organization's voice.

Compelling. Knowing what to do and wanting to do it are completely different things. A brand has to tap into the aspirations of the organization to affect behavior. People want to be part of something that matters. While you can build a working entity without a sense of compelling purpose, it won't become a great or enduring one.

Actionable Compelling True

Compelling brands aren't just inspiring to insiders. They are relevant, compelling, and exert a strong "pull" on target audiences outside of the organization.

True. The all-too-common public perception that brands are deceptive window dressing comes from the reality that short-term, actionable, and compelling brands can be effective posers. Think Enron. But if you want a better and enduring brand, build it on what's true.

True to the culture and capabilities of the organization. True to the on-the-ground realities of executing on promises. And especially true to the expectations of your outside audiences. Because sadly, some ideas, no matter how true, will never be believed.

An organization can talk about aspirations for its brand. But it needs to be careful not to overreach or become boastful.

1 + 1 + 1 = Better Brands. When a brand is actionable, compelling, and true it will become known for something important, instantly recognizable, and improve the organization's ability to compete.

Start here. Gather a cross-section of people within the organization to discuss how your brand is performing on these simple, but powerful measures. It's the first step on the path to Building Better Brands.

Building Better Brands That...

Building a better brand isn't its own reward. It creates an asset that drives choice and retention. Specifically, choice by the audiences you want to buy a product or service, support a cause, or change their behavior. And not just choice, but loyalty that ensures that once the brand wins you believers, you can hold onto them for the long term.

The mechanics of choice and retention are well understood. There are a series of "gates" that a target person passes through in a set order—awareness, familiarity, consideration, choice, and loyalty. The gates drive the sales and fulfillment process of entering a market, getting on the "long-list," surviving the winnowing down to the "short list," winning, and ultimately building loyalty.

When you build or evolve a brand that is optimized for all of the gates you will win more often and keep more of what you win.

The terminology used by experts may vary, but the underlying path is straightforward and undeniable. The real issue is, "How does a brand relate to each of these gates?" Once you understand the answer to that question you'll be ready to begin evaluating and improving a brand's performance at each stage of the journey.

AWARENESS

entry

FAMILIARITY

long-list

"Our task wasn't to teach leadership about branding. It was for us to determine how to leverage the brand assets of the corporation to win more often. Once we could do that, we had the attention of the C-suite."

—**CMO AT A GLOBAL TECHNOLOGY COMPANY**

CONSIDERATION	CHOICE	LOYALTY
short list	win	retain

Elements of Building Better Brands

Identity is the best understood brand element—and perhaps the most overrated. It is the brand name and logo. It is a unique color or sound that everyone comes to associate with one organization. It must be distinctive, memorable, protectable, and appropriate. It is what is noticed and remembered. It is the face of the brand.

It is possible to recognize a brand identity long before you know anything about what it means.

AWARENESS

entry

Arena is straightforward, but it is often overlooked. It is a statement of where the brand chooses to compete.

Defining a brand's competitive arena tells the world what you do and who are your competitors. It is the ring into which you have tossed your hat. A brand can't make the long-list unless it tells its markets where it competes.

Defining arena can be challenging for diversified corporations.

FAMILIARITY

long-list

Positioning is just what it sounds like—the relative relationship of a brand to its competitors. Getting short-listed requires communicating specific reasons (attributes) that are most important to a target audience.

Positioning gets tricky when you have diverse audiences who may have very different criteria for choice. "Drivers of choice" also change over time, which means that positioning must evolve as well.

CONSIDERATION

short list

Character is key to winning. Any audience that has progressed through the gates has vetted a short list of brands. Each can deliver what is needed. The remaining question is, "Who do I want to be associated with?"

It may be an issue of trust, or chemistry, or prestige—but the character of a brand is the most important gating factor in choice. As you can imagine, the more important the purchase or use—to life, limb, well-being, or pride—the more character matters.

CHOICE

win

Experience is undeniable. A consistent failure to deliver on a brand's promise will lead to its failure. That's why thinking through every aspect of the brand experience is so important.

Great brands develop and test comprehensive 'models' of their brand experience—listening carefully to the feedback of key audiences. They then re-engineer their operations, train their employees and partners, and evolve the real-world brand experience.

LOYALTY

retain

Our brand champions are constantly fighting the many tentacles of random acts of branding.

Champions

Meet Carol Gee, Carmenchu Mendiola-Fernández, and Van Perry. They are three of the many brand champions I've worked with to create and evolve brands.

Brand champions can have a profound influence on the business and brands of their organizations. They are the ones that have been driven, smart, and stubborn enough to find a path forward to a better brand.

Before you set out on your own journey to create or evolve a brand, Carol, Carmenchu, and Van have agreed to share some of the triumphs, challenges, and surprises that marked their efforts.

Carol Gee

Carol Gee led the team that rebranded $6.2 billion of DuPont's synthetic fibers businesses as INVISTA. She also headed the unification of Owen-Illinois' brand into a global platform befitting the largest glass bottle maker on earth.

Welcome Carol. What was the genesis of the INVISTA program?

Steve McCracken, SVP of DuPont and leader of the $6B fibers business encouraged DuPont to sell off its independent fibers businesses. He believed that a stand-alone company, dedicated to all the aspects of designing, making, supporting, and marketing synthetic fibers, would do far better than a collection of low-growth fibers businesses trapped inside of a diversified corporation like DuPont.

How did you get involved in such a major brand program?

I was the de facto corporate communications leader of the fibers businesses, in charge of a number of key brands, including LYCRA® fiber, COOLMAX® fabric, and CORDURA® fabric—so it made sense to involve me in the creation of a stand-alone fibers business. When Steve asked me to lead the creation of the brand for the new company I was thrilled. An adventure with Steve! But I had never done that before. I had never defined a company brand, only the brands for products.

Did your organization's leadership understand the importance, the difficulty, of what they were undertaking?

We were energized by the idea of having our own brand. It was going to be a chance to prove how good we could be. But we were also terrified of losing the power of the DuPont brand. Everyone knew how important the new brand would be to our success.

It's hard for leadership to see you as a business person, not just a branding person. The reason that we took so much care in finding the right partner to develop the program was to bring credibility to our team. We had to get this right the first time. The spin-off was huge—$6.2 billion worth of DuPont.

Fashion, carpeting, industrial fibers, chemistry—in addition to the marketers, many of our guys were hard-core engineers and scientists. Still, they got into it. It was interesting. Our people came with a sense of purpose. Fear helped, as we could not go back.

Much of the process was driven by our customers. We shaped the brand not just on our own desires and assets, but on what had meaning for them. That emboldened us.

While the brand development process went smoothly, keeping people focused was daunting. We had people worrying about losing their jobs, their pensions. Fear was there.

We tried to keep communicating about what we knew. But the unknown is the unknown. The IPO and spin-off process could have derailed the branding process. We deserve a medal for keeping things on track!

Tell us about the process.

We took pride in the process. Every step was real, not faux. We made sure it was steeped in truth.

We started with character. Character defines companies. Get that wrong and nothing can be true. We loved the character workshops. They made us reach deep and consider not just who we were, but who we were becoming. We knew where we came from as DuPont'ers but had to talk about our aspirations for where we wanted to go. The process forced us to ask the questions that you normally ignore, at your own peril!

What was most challenging element?

For us, choosing an arena was hard. We were four major divisions that were being put together to form a new company. Each was used to its own territory, its own arena. We had to decide what we were going to do together. The insight that we could become the only fully integrated synthetics fiber company "from the molecule to the market," was entirely new. Once we figured out that common ground, we had a key element to unify us.

The brand positioning was critical. We had to find a place in the market without the halo of the DuPont brand. The brand positioning had to be strong enough for us to stand alone. To properly position "NewCo" we pursued a depth of research—quantitative research—that we hadn't ever done before.

As a science-based company, that rigor was necessary to help us make decisions. We knew, with the global research, that we were properly defining the brand. What emerged was the understanding that the attribute, "Acts as a partner" was the number one driver of choice across all of our businesses. That, along with our unique ability to innovate, gave us the components to build a great brand.

How did you involve the broader organization?

Modeling the future of the brand—the experience—was key to our success. We had to show ourselves what we could look and sound like. That visualization of what you're creating is very important to the process. Everyone is from Missouri, the "Show-Me State." Once we could bring the future to life, people were inspired. Don't skip this step!

We modeled the experience before we finalized the name and logo. That was fine. Those identity elements are secondary to how you will define yourself, your character and arena. Everything can be built without a name. The name and logo were icing on the cake. Because we knew so clearly what we wanted to convey, we were able to create a corporate identity that was a personification of those ideas: a way to deliver it out into the world.

What surprised you most about the brand development process?

I was surprised by how the process fed on itself. Each stage was so well defined that it carried us to the next. As people follow that process, outlined in this book, they will also be surprised by how easily such a complex and daunting journey is completed.

Pitfalls?

Don't take shortcuts. Go through the process. Don't miss a step, you might miss the magic. The branding process is a journey of discovery that leads to creation. Listening, really listening, is critical. Picture yourself as a detective. Don't accept the first or most obvious solution.

Most important: Create something that isn't just compelling, make sure it is true. As you often told us, "If you want something that lasts, it has to be built on a compelling truth."

What did the brand program achieve?

For me, this was one of the greatest parts of my 40-year career. The day we launched INVISTA was inspiring. People around the world were thrilled. It was completely accepted. That was so gratifying! I often think about that moment. What we did for the organization. They deserved that joy—that name, that identity, that positioning to "Step Forward." DuPont also got a great price for the spin-off!

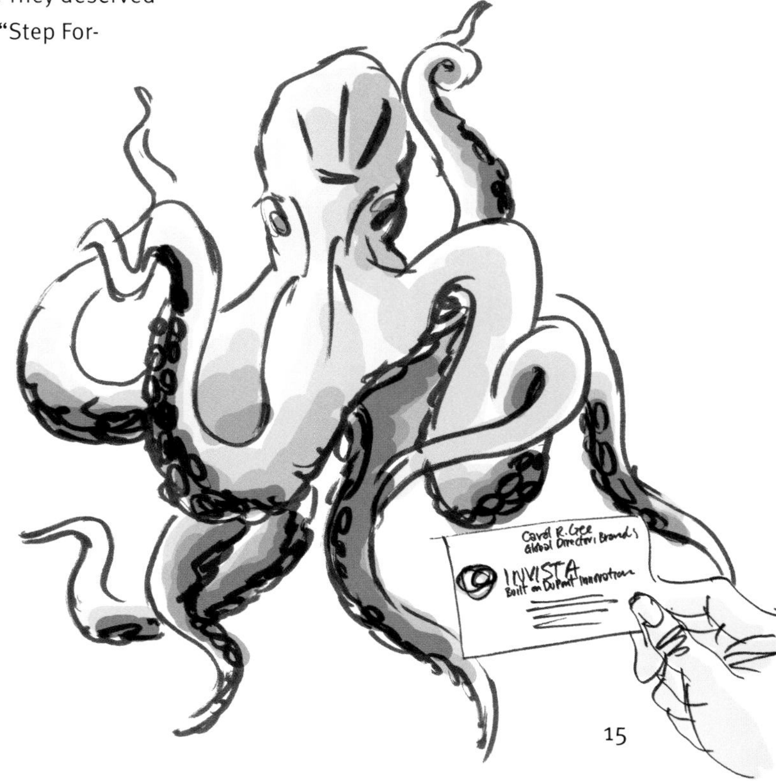

Carmenchu Mendiola-Fernández

Carmenchu Mendiola-Fernández led the team that recast the brand strategy and identity for TWC. The Washington Center for Internships and Academic Seminars provides students with transformational experiences that foster academic and professional achievement, leadership, and civic engagement.

You've been working to evolve The Washington Center (TWC) Brand for four years. How is it going?

It takes years to rethink and then build a brand. It's not just about the visual identity. It is in aligning what we do, what we say, and how we look. It's a process. Don't be in a hurry to finish it. It isn't an end; it's a start.

You were new to branding when you started. How did you end up leading the TWC program?

I actually had no experience in branding. I was not an executive with credibility. All I had were books! But I understood that we had to make The Washington Center brand better, stronger. We had changed so much since our founding, but our brand didn't reflect what we had become.

You have to be persistent. I didn't have any idea what it would take. I was determined to find a way and it transformed my career.

How so?

I've been promoted to the executive level—the first person in several years to "move up." That means I'm now part of most conversations that are about changing the organization. I'm a part of strategic planning. In the past, the communications group was there to make what was requested. Now we help shape what we say and do.

How did you build that credibility?

We met with everyone. We became good about bringing people together, bringing them into the process. Lots of showing, sharing, and patience.

We also used quick wins, pilot projects, to show that the new brand ideas would work. Work with the people that actually want to work with you, that believe in the brand promise. The others will follow.

How is the branding team seen today?

Four years ago I never would have thought people could see us as advisors, experts. Before, it was, "Make this," "Do this." Now, people expect us to integrate everything.

What surprised you most?

My surprise is that even though you are the same person working with the same executives you can completely change their perceptions. We can now accomplish things much faster. We have credibility.

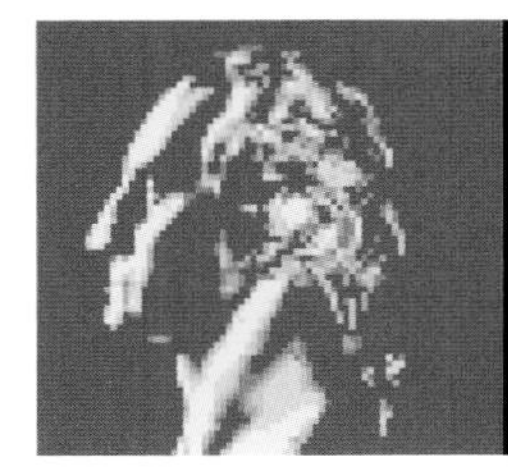

The Washington Center

Advice?

Documenting everything is important. You have to show people the progress you've made. That documentation is also critical to continuity. People come and go, but The Washington Center needs to stay true to its brand.

Also, make the time to properly map the journeys of your key audiences. That was hard for us to do—we were busy with our "day" jobs. We didn't realize how important it was until later.

What did the brand program achieve?

People have noticed the change in how we look. That's the most visible change. We do a far better job of explaining the value of TWC. We have won awards.

But the real change is in elevating and bringing consistency to everything we do. I got a call from the White House yesterday about inviting our students to attend an exclusive event. They and others are seeing and hearing about us in a more compelling way. Instead of just talking about how big or old we are, we are communicating the value of what we do. That's gaining us more supporters.

Internally, the ideas of the brand ring true. Understanding the brand and the customer journey has affected every part of the organization.

Walk us through the branding process.

The discovery process was very helpful. You're not just trying to position yourself in the best way, you are trying to be true to who you are, your history, your past. As we talked to people inside and out of TWC, we began to see what was possible, what we could really be.

Defining TWC's character helped us get to the core of who we were, who we are, and what we wanted to be. That had to come from us, not outsiders or consultants.

What made the most profound difference?

Positioning gave us focus and allowed us to prioritize our audiences. We learned to find the right balance, to coordinate our actions. That was new! We started to talk about the importance of the experience we create for students, not just the resources we had. That led to a positioning centered on our approach instead of our assets: "Experience that Transforms."

The move from a tangible, TWC-centric view to the idea of a student's experience was a huge leap. When we began to think about how we were relevant to our audiences—that changed everything.

What about the new identity?

You shouldn't change a logo just for the sake of change. For us, we needed to signal a break from the old. The change to a new look and feel really helped. It showed we were serious about the new brand positioning. People really like our new identity. It feels authentic.

Final thoughts?

Through the brand and its positioning you can become a "connector." Be passionate. Remain determined during the transition. Stay true to the brand!

Van Perry

Van, you were part of the creation of the first national bank brand. How did that start?

While there were many banks named "First National," there wasn't a single bank entity that spanned the United States prior to our launch of NationsBank. When Congress repealed the Glass-Steagall Act, that paved the way for the creation of banks that crossed state lines.

But the real force that transformed the North Carolina Savings Bank (NCNB) into NationsBank, then into the new Bank of America, was our CEO, Hugh McColl. He had an almost messianic ambition to build a great American bank.

Why were you chosen for that mission?

I was working as a development officer in an NCNB subsidiary. Our focus was community reinvestment, something I was well-prepared for given my MBA in Public Policy. I was approached by a director of marketing at the bank to lead a secret project: project "Warpaint."

Despite my lack of branding or identity training or experience, they felt my ability to organize and integrate complex projects would be valuable.

I took the job even though I was not sure where that decision would lead me. In fact, I was instructed not to tell my colleagues what new role I had accepted!

Did people understand the stakes?

There was no question that everyone at NCNB understood the importance of getting the right brand to fit the vision. But few had any idea of the effort that it would take.

Van Perry was the leader of the program that created NationsBank, and only seven years later, oversaw the rebranding of Bank of America brand (after its acquisition by NationsBank).

Hugh McColl was determined to remake banking on a national, even international level. A search was on for a major acquisition to intensify the expansion already underway in Texas and Florida. We needed to be ready.

Our management had also begun to understand that the NCNB brand would not necessarily work on a larger stage. As we moved into Texas, some had started to refer to NCNB as "No Cash for No Body!" That added even more urgency to our work.

So you built a new kind of bank brand, in secrecy; then seven years later, did it again. How many people were involved?

A small group can create a national brand. We started out as 2–3 people. As we got to implementation, we grew to 12–15. Of course many more helped, but a tiny core was able to lead the change in everything.

What it does require is that the branding team get "gold card" access. We had to borrow and steal resources from across the organization, sometimes without saying what it was for. But we had the blessing from our CEO.

Also, since this was a new brand, there was a hunger in the organization to understand where we were headed. We were the experts because we were creating the brand. We had the answers!

Did it go smoothly?

I was surprised at how chaotic it became. How fast everything changed. We thought we had a year, then suddenly a merger deal was made and we had only six months.

There are going to be unknowns. For us, timing was an unknown. How or when the C&S/Sovran acquisition would become integrated was an unknown. In fact, the NationsBank brand program was a contingency plan, put into stasis until the conditions were right.

What's key?

For us, brand strategy was the key. It brought everything and everyone together. The idea of "A national bank with a community spirit" was a clear guide to the name, logo, and marketing of NationsBank. You can even hear echoes of that theme in Bank of America's tagline, "Bank of Opportunity."

What did the brand program achieve?

The brand change to NationsBank, then to Bank of America was completely successful. Employees across the merged banks were engaged and understood the character and ideas of the emerging brand. There were no customer rebellions! We proved it was possible to create a national, then international, bank brand.

You didn't return to the real estate group following the introduction of NationsBank...

No, it seemed pedestrian to go back to my old role. Creating a new identity gives you access to senior leadership, to becoming a part of real change. I was hooked! So I moved forward and managed NationsBank's involvement in the 1996 Atlanta Olympics. Then in 1998 I again led the bank's effort when we acquired and rebranded Bank of America.

Any parting advice?

Surround yourself with good people you trust. Ask yourself, "Is this going to have value for the customer? Is this confusing?" That's a key question, a key guide. But don't just be market-driven; focus as much on the internal audiences as the customers.

Discovery

To build a better brand, you have to understand, completely, both the current situation and the shape of the future. The more thoroughly you investigate each element—identity, arena, positioning, character, and experience—the more likely you are to generate insights that lead to ambitious and profitable change.

This chapter appears early in the book because you must begin the brand development process with discovery. But you should read through all of the other chapters before you begin. Knowing how you will use what you discover will help you proceed with focus and confidence.

1. Map the Journey

It's important that you do your homework before developing a better brand. You will be tempted to survey the landscape from your own vantage point, but it's best to trek through an organization's chosen arena from the point of view of its audiences.

That means literally following the journey of each audience as they make their way through learning about, considering, choosing, and working with your organization. While there will be prominent features of the landscape that all may see, each audience takes its own path and has its own experience during the journey.

What does a prospective customer hear, see, and experience as they seek a partner, provider, product, or service? What about a prospective employee? Or an investor? Your challenge is to "map the journey," audience by audience. A kind of "year in the life of..." documentary. Once you've sketched the routes, go even deeper.

- Collect marketing and communications encountered along the way.
- Analyze current strategic plans to understand how they may change the landscape.
- Review research that reveals how audiences are making decisions.
- Talk to the people who shape the organization, its products, and its services.
- Study peers and competitors.
- Consider whether there are pending mergers or acquisitions, global trends, or cultural upheavals that will shift the balance of power in the industry.
- Weigh how changes in leadership will influence the way the organization functions or approaches the market.

*work*PLAN

1. Map the journey
2. Review strategic documents
3. Analyze existing research
4. Poll influencers
5. Interview key constituencies
6. Visit stores, facilities, offices

Audience journey maps need to capture stages that represent the state of mind of the traveler.

Learn

Choose

Interact

Bond

A traditional marketing and communications audit focuses on gathering the printed and online materials that are used throughout an organization. A more thorough audit effort will obtain photos of signs and facilities. But you can do better.

Gather materials—not just from your organization, but from primary competitors. And think beyond basic marketing and communications. The goal is to have a clear view of everything meaningful that each audience sees, hears, and experiences over an extended period.

The advantage of approaching this as a journey is that you'll gather intelligence on elements you'd otherwise miss. For example, what do prospective employees see as they arrive at the interview site? How are they greeted by security personnel or the receptionist? Are they given a form to fill out? What does that form look like? What do applicants do if they have questions? What are they thinking along the way? You get the idea.

By putting yourself in the shoes of employees, customers, partners, channel representatives, analysts, and others you can walk through their entire experience, gathering, annotating, and photographing along the way.

Segment those journeys in a logical way. First, an audience learns about your organization and competitors. Then they collect information about contenders to consider and choose who is the best fit. Once they've decided, they interact with the organization and its product or services, including things like instructions for use, repairs, returns, career development, etc. Finally, there are moments of bonding, when a problem is fixed, special rewards are earned, or a relationship is forged that goes beyond a mere transactional exchange.

Learn, choose, interact, bond, it isn't just a linear journey, it's a cycle that repeats over and over again.

DISCOVERY *work*PLAN

1. Map the journey
2. Review strategic documents
3. Analyze existing research
4. Poll influencers
5. Interview key constituencies
6. Visit stores, facilities, offices

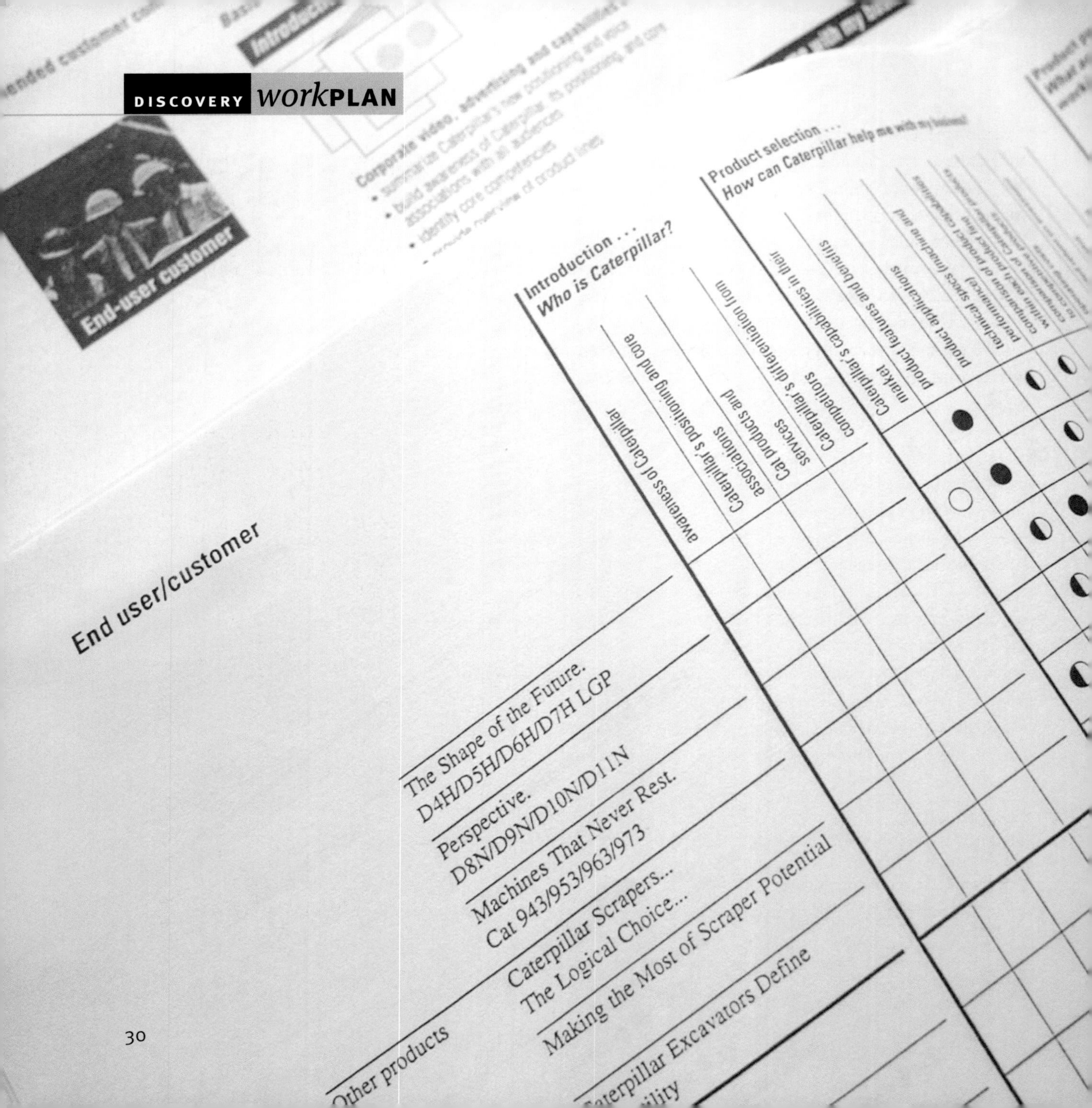

End-user customer
Corporate video, advertising and capabilities
summarize Caterpillar's new positioning and voice
build awareness of Caterpillar, its positioning, and core associations with all audiences
identify core competencies
End user/customer
Introduction . . .
Who is Caterpillar?
awareness of Caterpillar
Caterpillar's positioning and core associations
Cat products and services
Caterpillar's differentiation from competitors
Product selection . . .
How can Caterpillar help me with my business?
Caterpillar's capabilities in their market
product features and benefits
product applications
technical specs (machine and performance)
comparison of product capabilities within each product line
The Shape of the Future.
D4H/D5H/D6H/D7H LGP
Perspective.
D8N/D9N/D10N/D11N
Machines That Never Rest.
Cat 943/953/963/973
Caterpillar Scrapers...
The Logical Choice...
Making the Most of Scraper Potential
Caterpillar Excavators Define
Other products

To catalog the journey of key audiences, it is best to observe them as they learn, choose, interact, and bond with the organization and competitors. You'll be surprised by how much you didn't know about their experience. It's useful to create an inventory for each audience organized by the questions that they need answered like, "How can you help me with my business?", "Can I buy your products and services as bundles?", etc. Getting into their heads will allow you to become far more responsive and relevant.

The journey maps you build at this stage will not only be useful now, they'll prove to be invaluable guides in upcoming stages of the brand development process.

In this example, the journey was structured by posing a series of questions and identifying corresponding content needs.

The team then inventoried existing materials and assessed whether they fully or partially met each audience's needs along the way.

DISCOVERY

*work*PLAN

1. Map the journey
2. Review strategic documents
3. Analyze existing research
4. Poll influencers
5. Interview key constituencies
6. Visit stores, facilities, offices

DISCOVERY *work*PLAN

Sometimes the easiest way to map the journey is to trek it yourself. Here, the vast NYC public transportation system was captured through the eyes and minds of the riders—a perspective that spurred a system wide remaking of the MTA brand.

The new brand strategy and identity were tied to substantive changes in the quality of the rider experience and the introduction of the MetroCard®—an electronic fare system that brought a new cohesiveness to moving through the subways, buses, trains, bridges, and tunnels that comprise the MTA system.

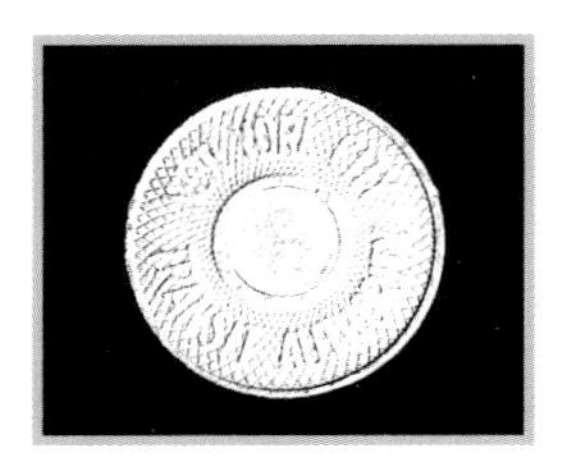

DISCOVERY

*work*PLAN

1. Map the journey
2. Review strategic documents
3. Analyze existing research
4. Poll influencers
5. Interview key constituencies
6. Visit stores, facilities, offices

rmany
USA
The Moorings Mainsheet
Sailing in Paradise
Discover Your Perfect Vacation!
Aller guten Dinge
le boat
European Boating Vacations
TUI Experiences
Туда, где Вы еще не бывали!
Sunsail
Traumhafte Bootsferien
boot
f.re.e
One Week from $300
NEW! Springtime Sailing Offers!
One Week from $281
Discover Europe in a New Way!
The Moorings
29TH
INTERLINE
REGATTA
October 12 - 21, 2010
GRAND PRIZE
Call us about Race & Spectator Packages: 1-800-633-7348
www.TheMooringsInterlineRegatta.com
WATERLINES
Reef Weeks
25%
OCEAN ADVENTURES!
Unforgettable Adventure BVI
Getaways
NEW FOR 2010
$699
Beautiful Boating Vacations...

It helps to have a workroom with long walls to organize materials. Here, an organization takes advantage of windowed room dividers.

DISCOVERY *work*PLAN

1. Map the journey
2. Review strategic documents
3. Analyze existing research
4. Poll influencers
5. Interview key constituencies
6. Visit stores, facilities, offices

Is the plan to cruise ahead, enter new territories, or take drastic measures to correct course?

Are product or geographic divisions beginning to rise or fall in importance? Will the organizational structure evolve to meet new needs?

Will the organization grow organically, or are there substantive mergers and acquisitions on the horizon?

Have competitors emerged that are scrambling the established order? Or is your organization the upstart that is rewriting the rules?

Is leadership pursuing an ordered handoff of power from one generation to the next, or is the nature of who and what comes next uncertain?

2. Review Strategic Documents

Brands are not just a reflection of the past and present, they are the advance guard of the future.

Your brief is to capture a view of the entire organization's take on the future. Questions, such as those posed at left, can be answered by reviewing strategic planning documents.

In smaller "seat-of-the-pants" organizations you may find that little is written down. Outside sources, such as analysts' reports or "insider" blogs, may be of more use in profiling the arena and identifying trends, as well as offering plausible speculation on what is to come.

And while we will discuss how to analyze research and interview key people in the following pages—you'll find that those efforts are very much a part of understanding the strategic direction and goals of the organization.

Don't be concerned (or surprised) if there are inherent contradictions in strategic planning documents, five-year plans, annual report declarations, and outsider views of the best path forward. The goal of this step in the discovery process is to survey and summarize how the future is seen from each point of view, not to rationalize opposing viewpoints.

This part of discovery is less about the questions you are asking, and more about observing the essential questions the organization and the industry are asking themselves.

DISCOVERY

*work*PLAN

1. Map the journey
2. Review strategic documents
3. Analyze existing research
4. Poll influencers
5. Interview key constituencies
6. Visit stores, facilities, offices

You should look at research not only through expert and analytical eyes, but also through the eyes of the organization. While those views may be similar, they are more likely to reveal fundamental differences.

3. Analyze Research

Most organizations conduct research of one kind or another: anthropological research that provides an observed view of how people actually behave; qualitative research that provides clues and spurs ideas but offers no statistical certainty; quantitative research that is designed to provide a predictive view of how larger groups think and will behave; and occasionally, census research that attempts to poll each and every member of a specialized group (or cohort).

Whatever the methodology, the intent is to increase understanding of what is and what may be. The more rigorous the methodology and larger the sample size, the greater confidence you can have in the results.

Gather and analyze existing research studies, but be careful. Given the technical nature of research study design, a layperson can easily give too much credence to the findings of a flawed global quantitative study or too little consideration to a small, elegantly fielded anthropological effort. You may need some very specialized help to interpret what you're reading.

But even if you decide you need a research expert, you can do a preliminary analysis of your own. Remember, you want to accomplish two goals. The more obvious one is to mine the data to understand what they reveal. But an equally important goal is to see the research and its conclusions through the eyes of the organization as a whole.

In research-savvy cultures, reality and perception may be aligned. But in some organizations, research is a poorly vetted, thinly-veiled justification to support partisan views. Part of your job is to clarify whether existing research is sound or suspect.

Whatever the quality or quantity of existing research, pull out the key questions that are being asked. Note how audiences are segmented and described and which "attributes" are being measured—such as "provides responsive services," "acts like a partner," and "drives innovation in the industry." Those building blocks of performance will be important to the brand positioning work you'll be doing later.

DISCOVERY

*work*PLAN

1. Map the journey
2. Review strategic documents
3. Analyze existing research
4. Poll influencers
5. Interview key constituencies
6. Visit stores, facilities, offices

Lions, pundits, and bears. Oh my!

While the predictions of market lions and bears, as well as pundits, are notoriously unreliable, they do profoundly shape the course of industries, businesses, and brands.

4. Poll Influencers

You may have noticed that we're working our way through primarily secondary sources—communications and marketing materials, strategic documents, and research—before we talk directly with people. This approach allows us to gain a deep understanding of what exists, before delving into what was intended. Once you meet the people behind what's happening, you may be influenced by their perceptions of what's been accomplished.

Before you move to primary sources, take time to listen to the influencers. They are the lions of the industry, the pundits who spin, and the Cassandras, real or false, who preach decline. Their role, often their job, is to shape what happens by predicting the future. The most objective of influencers (often the very best journalists) strive to let their investigations lead where they may. The worst, and unfortunately sometimes the most persuasive of the influencers, have a theme or story line they want to advance. Facts, if contrary, be damned!

As with analyzing research, yours is a dual role. First, search for the truth in what influencers are saying. Where is the industry headed and why? Where are the opportunities and pitfalls? Who is seen as best positioned for the future and why?

Second, describe and analyze the trends and how they have affected your organization and the broader market. What is the mood and what are the myths that are driving people's perceptions? A cogent synthesis of prevailing opinions is a valuable guide to the forces that are part of the brand landscape.

1. Map the journey
2. Review strategic documents
3. Analyze existing research
4. Poll influencers
5. Interview key constituencies
6. Visit stores, facilities, offices

Beyond superb preparation, here are some keys to great interviews.

Unless the interviewee is the CEO or someone who speaks with complete impunity, promise (and deliver) anonymity.

Ask for a personal view. Tell people that you've read much of what's been published by and about the organization. You understand the official and public view; and you need their unique perspective and insight.

Remember you are there to learn and to build bridges. Both are equally important. An interview should be the first of many conversations, not the last.

Take careful notes with a pen and paper (or at least stylus and tablet). Clicking keyboards are not welcome here. Good notes capture ideas and verbatim statements of import.

You can complete lists and fix spellings of names later. Focus on what's important.

Never take a superior to a subordinate's interview.

Consider bringing a second, unobtrusive note taker, so you can concentrate on the discussion. But still take your own critical notes. That's respectful (and prudent).

Type up your notes as soon as possible. The same day is best. It will fix concepts in your mind and ensure that notes are legible and accessible for your core team.

5. Interview Key Constituencies

If you have done a thorough job with discovery, you should have learned an immense amount about the organization, key constituencies, competitors, industry, and available information and trends shaping all of those elements. You are now ready to talk with the people that matter most: the leaders, long-term employees, newbies, up-and-comers, and even troublemakers within the organization.

Be confident in your approach. Given your hard-won knowledge, you are no longer a mere petitioner asking for a bit of insider wisdom. You are a source of intelligence and perspective on what's happening—and what may happen next. An example: Two oil-exploration executives once laughingly asked me why they should waste their time talking to a brand expert—they were doing more than fine. My response? "I understand your company is no longer the first choice for new engineering talent—What's changed?" It was the start of a candid and productive conversation.

Many interviews are easy. You tell the person you are there to understand the organization—what drives its people, what the firm does like no other, where the industry is headed—and an hour later you're suggesting setting up a follow-up discussion. Other interviews may start slowly, haltingly. Some people may be suspicious of your motives or insecure in their positions.

The better you know the organization and the background of the people you're interviewing, the easier it is to find the trigger that gets them talking. Everyone has a trigger. Don't be afraid to be provocative if you must, but always be respectful.

Get to the heart of what matters with interviews and you'll gain real insight and supporters. But get the facts right or you will be summarily dismissed.

1. Map the journey
2. Review strategic documents
3. Analyze existing research
4. Poll influencers
5. Interview key constituencies
6. Visit stores, facilities, offices

You should try to ask these essential questions in the interviews.

What is at the core of your organization? How did it begin?

What stories, even myths, have shaped its purpose and culture?

What are the most significant forces reshaping the industry, competitors, and your organization?

Where do you choose to compete and how is that changing?

Who are your key audiences and what drives them to choose you (or competitors)?

Does the organization's reputation reflect its true strengths?

What distinguishes you from competitors and up-and-comers?

Who are you, how do you act as a culture? Has that changed over the years?

Does the organizational character have to evolve further?

Does the organization deliver on what is promised?

Does the name, logo, design, sound, and style of communications and marketing fit the organization?

Tailor your interviews to the person. The CFO, CMO, line manager, and sales representative will expect you to probe for insight in their areas of expertise. Listen to what they say, adjust your approach and tone to ensure they feel comfortable and get a chance to express their issues and hopes for the organization.

The circumstances of the brand program will also affect the interviews. If the impetus is a pending merger, the focus of the questions will be very different than a brand project spurred by the rise of a new competitor.

Despite the differences in the perspectives of the people you'll interview, there are a handful of essential questions you should try to ask. The answers will provide a basis for the core ideas that will define the brand.

As you read through the rest of this book you'll better understand what information you need to glean from the interviews.

DISCOVERY

*work*PLAN

1. Map the journey
2. Review strategic documents
3. Analyze existing research
4. Poll influencers
5. Interview key constituencies
6. Visit stores, facilities, offices

Williams
USA

6. Visit Facilities

If you want to judge an industrial construction company's ability to manage complex projects, visit its work sites. Are they organized and calm? Need to gauge the ability of a consultancy to scale and endure? Listen to how the power-players, the rainmakers, talk to subordinates (when they don't know you're watching). Skeptical of a company's ability to focus their talent and resources on what's vital to the future? Hang out in the employee cafeteria for a few afternoons. You'll soon know the truth.

Get away from the corporate HQ into the hinterlands. Note the language used to describe strategic imperatives. See how things really work. Do the same—as much as possible—with competitors. There's no substitute for field work.

This last stage of discovery combines elements of all the others. It is the part of the journey that provides a ground-level view of reality. Interviewing people in situ lets people relax and show you how things work.

DISCOVERY

*work*PLAN

1. Map the journey
2. Review strategic documents
3. Analyze existing research
4. Poll influencers
5. Interview key constituencies
6. Visit stores, facilities, offices

WORDLY
TRUSTWORTHY
INVENTIVE
$ £ € ¥
IRREVERENT
CREATIVE
BRILLIANT
STYLISH
ACCESSIBLE
ECLECTIC

Character

Brands with clearly defined character are recognized for how they behave, not just their name or logo.

Audiences experience brands by moving through the gates of choice. But crafting the elements that define each gate needs to be done in a different order.

As shown below, we need to understand character before we make choices about where and how we go to market. And identity isn't a driver of brands, it is a container of brand meaning whose definition is best left for last.

In the following chapters we will step through each element that needs to be defined to build better brands.

Character

Arena

Start With Character

While the "gates" or stages leading to choice and loyalty run in a set order, the development of brand elements doesn't follow the same logic.

Character, not identity, comes first because it drives all of the choices made by the organization. Then **arena**, as it defines the playing field and dictates who you are trying to reach. Third, **positioning**, which determines your strategy for appealing to the key audiences. Next? A modeling of the desired **experience**, because it is the stage where the full brand story unfolds. And finally, **identity**, because its form should be honed to fit the other brand elements, not the other way around.

When you know who you are, it becomes far easier to make decisions—about everything. That's true for people and brands. Should our logo (or employees) be bold? Ingenious? Cautious? Where should we extend our services? Is it appropriate for us to partner with...? You get the idea.

The brands that are most successful—the ones you admire the most—are predictable (or predictably unpredictable). You understand their character, so you have a good sense of how they will act, sound, feel, and even smell.

Rugged
Experienced
Powerful

CATERPILLAR®

Practical
Straightforward
Ingenious

A cool Microsoft product.

A Jacuzzi toilet.

A revolutionary Dyson dishwasher.

A dirty McDonalds.

A Harley made by AMF.

What's In Character?

Consider each of the statements at left. You probably scoffed at some, were sure of the veracity of others, and were positive that a few were outright lies. (Only one statement isn't at least occasionally true.)

It's remarkable how good we are at knowing what is on- or off-brand; in gauging what's absolutely true or sort-of-true or at least might-someday-be-true. That includes a pitch-perfect sense of what's right (or wrong) for everything from the design of products, to the way a company gets things done, to the focus of the people in charge.

Unfortunately, we're often tone deaf when it comes to our own companies and brands. It's hard to imagine that anyone at Harley-Davidson thought that AMF, a world leader in bowling equipment, should control their company. Or for that matter, that Avon believed they were the right people to own Tiffany. There were sound financial reasons for both transactions, but anyone thinking critically about character would have found other suitors. As you can easily imagine, both deals had to be unraveled to save these legendary brands.

The best brands have a way of building true faith in their character. While we all know that there must be a dirty McDonalds out there, we are sure that it is an outlier. Perhaps a smiling, mop-topped Ronald will be dispatched to set them straight!

Think about your own company or organization. Does everyone who works there know what's in character and what's not? Are discussions about everything—product development, hiring, acquisitions, the tone and language of communications, and more—grounded by a shared sense of "who we are and what we do"? They should be. As your organization grows it becomes even more important to define character.

Start-ups and small-businesses are cohesive by nature. Everyone knows everyone and has been part of creating the founding character of the place.

All brands evolve over time. It's the only way to stay relevant. But "How fast?" and "How far?" are important questions to discuss before taking the leap.

Imagine your current organization at twice or even 100 times the size. Spread across the globe. Adding people and even other organizations to the mix. How will you retain your integrity, your sense of self and purpose? How can you trust others who don't know who you are and what you stand for?

Changes in leadership and the disruption of established industries can also affect character. So don't assume that discussions of character are a once-in-a-blue-moon task. Character does evolve slowly. But like everything else in the world today, it evolves much faster than ever before.

By the way, Dyson doesn't (yet) design and make revolutionary dishwashers.

What separates one person from the next, one organization from the next? Character. While there are many ways to define character, I recommend choosing three traits. Why three? It forces you to make hard and *precise* choices. Three carefully chosen traits will allow you to foster consistent behavior without writing endless rules.

As you strive to define the evolving nature of a brand, shift and adjust the three traits until they interact in just the right way—capturing a truth that will guide everything the organization says and does. The combinations and permutations are nearly endless. So you're unlikely to ever find two companies with identical characters.

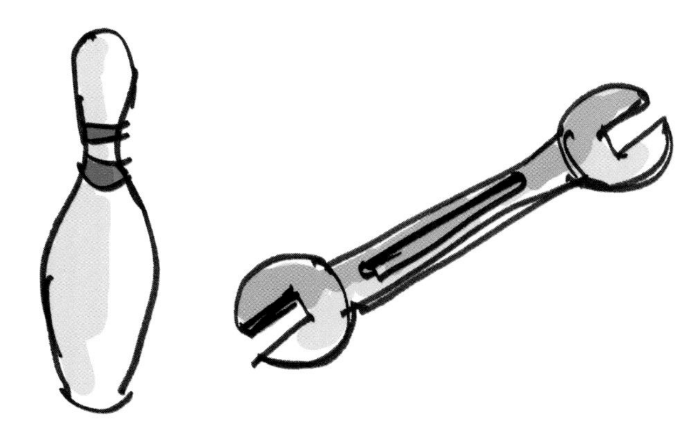

Each trait is critical. Imagine a person that is driven and charismatic. Those two characteristics give them the ability to spur others to action. But will they exploit their intrinsic strengths for good or evil? Selfish or selfless purpose? A third trait, just the right modifier—such as “narcissistic” or “giving”—is needed to truly understand how they will act.

You have to wonder why anyone thought that AMF would be the right parent company for Harley-Davidson.

Defining Character

To define the character of your organization you'll need to gather the right people, provide a clear framework, and facilitate the process.

Who should be part of the process?

Ultimately, everyone. But to get started, gather a small group that represents the heritage, current drivers, and up-and-comers of the organization. If a single gathering is not feasible, conduct a series of mini-workshops that move across the organization. Consolidate the results. You can also interview individuals, visit the archives, and conduct surveys to add richness and depth to the process.

The Rule of Three.

In the end there can be only three. Three character traits that together capture the evolving nature of the organization.

Why only three? As noted earlier, it forces you to make hard choices. No endless lists that everyone can agree to but no one uses. Three words are memorable and actionable. And three traits are enough to express a complex character. Get them just right and everyone will see the true nature of the organization in an elegant triad.

Facilitating

Your job is to keep everyone honest. Challenge platitudes. You're not looking to mindlessly reproduce an existing values statement. But be respectful. Character traits that might seem negative now may have been exactly right for a pioneering organization.

The hardest part is to keep everyone focused on the character of the organization—not just on traits that they personally have or admire. Imagine if the organization had a personality that you could describe to a friend—it does and you can!

NO. NO. NO! YOU ONLY GET 3. 3 THAT WORK TOGETHER. 3 THAT REFLECT YOUR HERITAGE, PRESENT, AND ASPIRATIONS.

Use Interactive Media

Find a big blank wall or a series of large windows. Set three zones—past, present, and future. Provide everyone with genuine 3"× 3" Post-it® Notes (the imitators fall off!) and bold black markers. With these simple tools, you can create a massive interactive environment to explore and define the organization's character.

Document the Process

Not everyone can be a part of the workshop. Take photos of each step's artifacts, take notes on the discussion, even film the process. When you meet with others, don't just share your conclusions, show them how a respected group of peers worked together to get to the right answers.

There are eight steps to defining brand character. Begin with a discussion of goals, process, and ground rules. Then engage the group in brainstorming. Get them to contribute their individual perspectives on how the brand character has evolved over time and where it is headed.

The workshop is structured to ensure that quieter voices are not drowned out and that every idea, even unpopular ones, have a chance to be heard. The result will be a broad and deep set of brand character traits: dozens, perhaps hundreds, of individual words printed on Post-it Notes.

The middle section, steps 3, 4, and 5, are all about bringing order to the chaos, making sense of the sea of words. You'll be amazed at how quickly and easily patterns and then ideas will emerge.

Step 6, "Craft," will be harder. It's here that the group must bring absolute clarity to the brand character. The constraint of three traits will force the group to reach genuine agreement—not simply negotiate a compromised laundry list of words.

The first six steps are designed to get the group to identify traits that are true, not ones selected to support a personal agenda.

In step 7, you will turn the discussion toward the implications of the character triad they've crafted. How would an organization with those traits act? What would it make? How would it look and feel? If the character definition leads to the wrong kind of behavior—or, just as problematic, doesn't seem actionable—you'll have to backtrack!

Last, you'll finalize the session's work, capturing the meaning and implications of the character traits.

CHARACTER *work*SHOP

1. Frame
2. Brainstorm
3. Organize
4. Characterize
5. Distill
6. Craft
7. Validate
8. Finalize

The setup for the workshop is simple. You'll want a comfortable space—preferably with windows. There must be either a broad set of windows or large enough wall space to display and arrange three distinct sets of dozens of Post-its.

Plan on about two hours (although you may want to combine this with other workshops outlined in this book into a full-day event).

Each participant will need a 3" × 3" pad of Post-its® and a bold, thin, black marker.

Designate a photographer to document the process and stages of development and a scribe to take detailed notes of the discussion.

1. Frame

The goal of the workshop is simple but profound. The group is going to define the character of the organization. Character defines actions and aspirations. It colors language and style. It isn't an affectation; it is an inherent truth that springs from heritage and desire. It evolves slowly.

Open a discussion about the inherent character of businesses and brands they know. Which seem sharp and genuine? How does that character affect the look, feel, sound, and actions of those organizations? Are there instances when a brand has done something that seems out of character?

Have some fun with "brand disconnects." Ask participants to propose the most wrong-headed character manifestations they can imagine—like a certain famous mouse smoking a cigar, a cluttered Apple store, grown men wearing red pigtailed wigs to promote Wendy's... Turn the discussion to your brand. Is its character well-defined? Has it been in flux? What is driving its evolution—new talent, competitive forces, growth? What excites them or worries them about the current or emerging character?

What about competitors? Have the group identify and define their primary character traits.

It may help to visualize a networking event where industry brands have gathered. You're acting as a guide for a good friend who is searching for a job. How would you describe each brand in the room? Remember, you're talking with a trusted friend, so choose revealing words such as "cutthroat," not code words like "challenging."

Now that the group is engaged and has a sense of the nature and purpose of brand character, the workshop can begin.

FUTURE

NIMBLE
AMBITIOUS
CLEVER

2. Brainstorm

Set up three sections—past, present, and future—on a broad wall or set of windows. The goal of the brainstorming session is to fill each section with traits that capture the character of the organization over time.

It's important that each participant gets a chance to consider and contribute a personal view without being influenced or pressured by others. To ensure that happens, give the group 20 minutes to quietly create their own stacks of character traits. They can draft as many Post-it Notes as needed for the past, present, and future zones. Each trait should be neatly written on an individual Post-it.

The past traits may be based on personal experience or myth. Whatever the participant believes was true. Don't be surprised if each participant's view of the present differs. Tenure, position, function, geography, and other factors all influence perceptions.

The future zone is for character traits that are emerging because of new leadership and talent, acquisitions and mergers, or aspirations for the evolution of the organization.

Once the group has had time to make their stacks of traits, ask them to put them all up in the past, present, and future sections. Take a few minutes to have everyone review the three collections of traits.

Give people about 20 minutes to create their three stacks of past, present, and future Post-its.

For startups, just choose present and future traits.

Use words that describe character traits. For example, "inexpensive" is a product attribute, "cheap" is a character trait.

Use clear and singular traits. Words like "integrity" represent bundles of traits like, "honest," "steadfast," "dependable," "selfless," etc. Create Post-its for each of the root traits.

integrity
DEPENDABLE
STRATEGIC
honest
Caring
TRUSTWORTHY
RESPONSIBLE
ACCESSIBLE
SAFE

3. Organize

At first, the three arrays of past, present, and future traits may seem overwhelming. But you'll soon find order in the chaos.

Divide the participants into three teams—past, present, and future. Each team should arrange the Post-it Notes in their section—stacking duplicates and grouping words with related meaning.

For example, the team at right grouped "integrity," "honest," "trustworthy," "responsible," and "caring."

It's likely that five or so groupings will emerge from dozens, even hundreds of traits. If there are too many, enlist the best wordsmiths from the teams to pack them more tightly.

This team decided to color-code their past, present, and future Post-its. That's a great way to keep things organized.

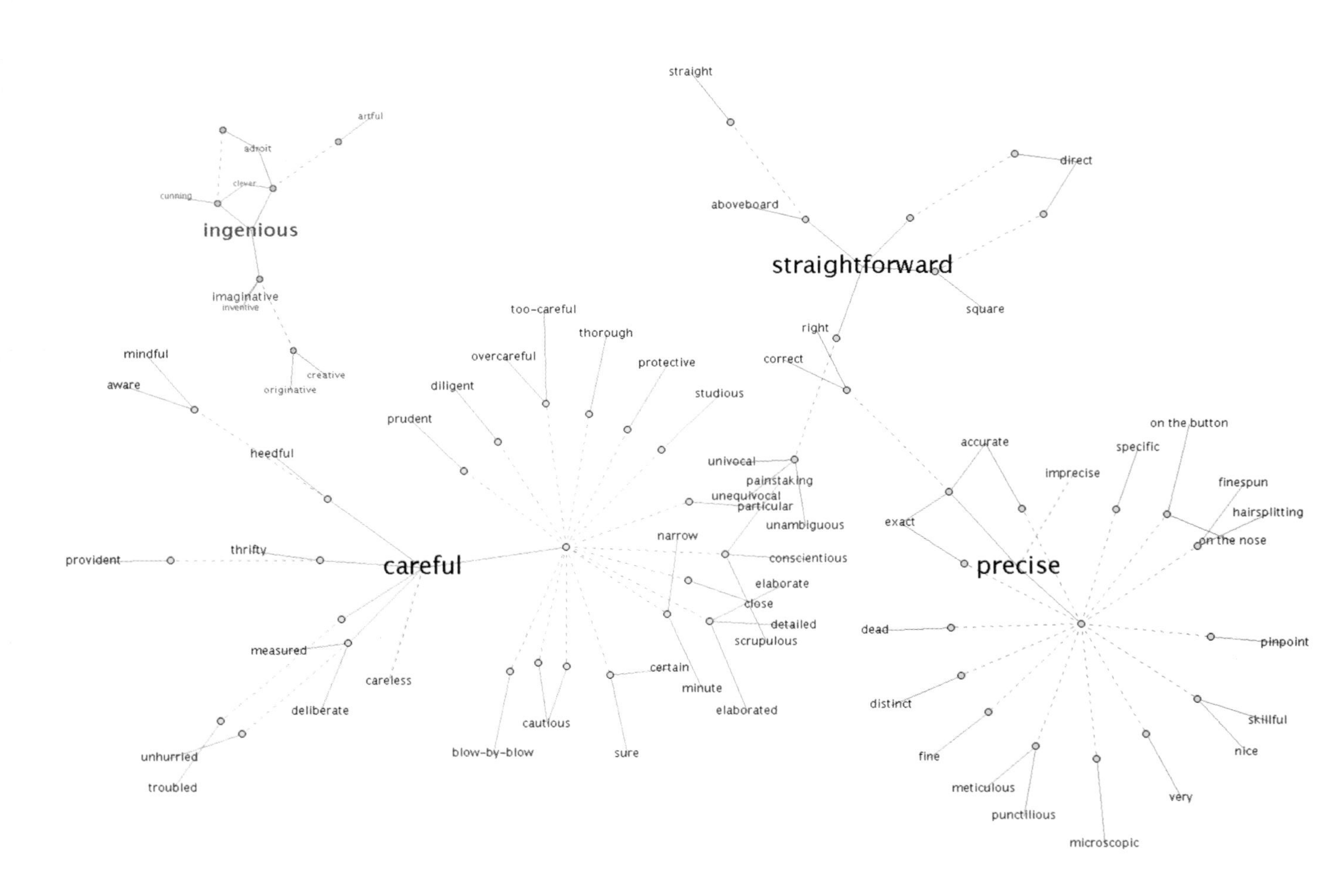
straight
artful
adroit
clever
cunning
ingenious
direct
aboveboard
straightforward
imaginative
inventive
square
too-careful
thorough
right
mindful
creative
originative
overcareful
protective
correct
aware
diligent
studious
prudent
on the button
accurate
specific
heedful
univocal
imprecise
painstaking
finespun
unequivocal
particular
hairsplitting
unambiguous
exact
narrow
on the nose
thrifty
provident
careful
conscientious
precise
elaborate
close
detailed
dead
scrupulous
pinpoint
measured
certain
careless
minute
distinct
deliberate
elaborated
cautious
skillful
unhurried
blow-by-blow
sure
fine
nice
troubled
meticulous
very
punctilious
microscopic

4. Characterize

Step back and the traits on the wall (or windows) will begin to tell a story. The groupings now represent coherent clusters of ideas. Label each group of traits with the word that best characterizes them as a whole.

For example, a group of words like, "adaptable, flexible, nimble, flighty, fickle" might be labeled "ADAPTABLE."

Step back again. The group can now scan across the past, present, and future and get a sense of the most prominent traits and the evolution of the organization's character over time. Together they begin to tell a story.

There are some typical patterns to look for. Pioneering organizations will often characterize the past in bold, even reckless terms—seeing the present as too conservative. There is sometimes an aspiration to return to some of the energy of the past, but in a more disciplined way.

Companies in crisis may characterize the present in very unflattering terms. And even thriving organizations will want to keep growing and evolving.

Identify and discuss the themes and shifts you see emerging on the wall.

These word diagrams were generated with Thinkmap's Visual Thesaurus. It's a great tool for brainstorming traits and can also help in finding the right synonym to use to characterize each group of traits. www.visualthesaurus.com

For the more hands-on, bringing several copies of the classic Roget's Thesaurus is highly recommended.

NIMBLE

5. Distill

Distillation is critical. It eliminates the extraneous and retains only the essence. In this step, the group will begin to make hard choices about what should define the organization's character going forward.

That character can't be completely aspirational, nor can it be entirely dictated by the past. One course would be a fantasy, the other would describe a museum.

What you're striving for is the perfect blend of tradition, current reality, and aspiration.

This needs to be an open discussion. Using the headings you've created for the groupings of traits, weigh what should be retained from the past and present. If it is possible, shed outdated or unproductive baggage. But decide what should never change.

Only consider future, aspirational traits that you believe are possible for the organization to embrace.

Pull out at least three and as many as seven key traits.

In this step we ask people to be advocates for key traits. As a moderator, make sure that everyone is heard.

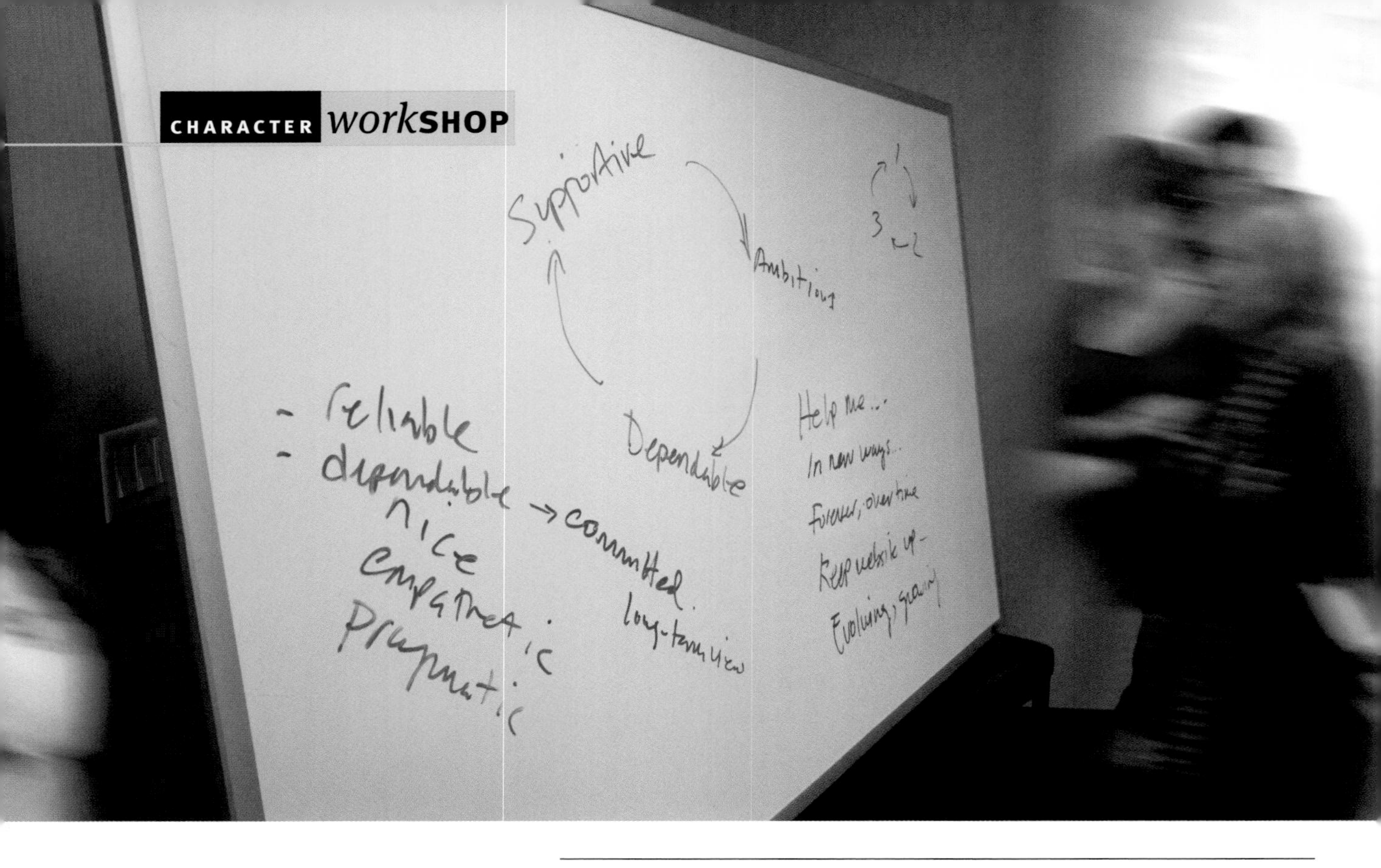

This group's participants felt that they had gotten their organization's first two traits exactly right—that its explosive nature was what fueled its innovative spirit. They then concentrated on tweaking the third trait to accurately reflect their close connection to others.

Make sure that everyone is fully engaged in the process of crafting the right combination of traits. You don't need complete agreement on the exact words.

It is common for a few people to prefer an alternative synonym. Listen to make sure that the core ideas are embraced—once you have that kind of consensus, you can move forward.

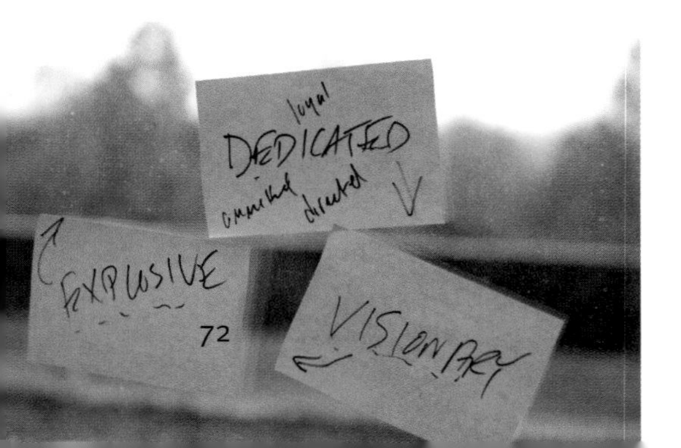

6. Craft

In this step, the group will decide on three traits that capture the truth about where the organization comes from and what it's becoming.

Find a clear spot to work with the key traits you've distilled from the past, present, and future. Some groups, like the one at left, move to a whiteboard for this part of the process. Do whatever works best for you.

Select three traits. Put them close together in a triangle. Consider their interaction. They should not be duplicative or overlap in meaning. They should affect each other. For example, "ambitious" could be seen as selfish, but add "supportive" and you begin to see it as "ambitious for others."

Try different combinations of the key traits. If you have more than three from the "distill" step, try different combinations. Remember, there can be only three!

Tweak the words themselves. A synonym with a slightly different emphasis might be exactly what's needed.

When you get all three right it will just "click."

Some hints:

- There is almost always a trait that spurs action or provides energy. The nature of that energy depends on the organization. For example, the traits "bold" or "fearful" both lead to action.
- A balanced character profile should make sense from all points of view. Consider whether the traits lean too much toward what is relevant either inside or outside.
- The final traits are meant to guide and inspire action. Choose pungent, strong words. Too many organizations feel they have to use sanitized language. If the words are watered-down, the brand will be watered-down.
- Be genuine.

START

7. Validate

The best test of character traits is to imagine putting them to use.

Discuss what the organization would do and say if it fully embraced the three traits you have chosen. What would the organization look like, sound like? How would it affect the development of products and services, recruiting and career paths?

What would the organization stop doing? Start doing? Do more of?

If the character isn't actionable or seems to drive the wrong kind of behavior, you don't have it right yet. Go back to step 6, "Craft."

This group was made up of people with diverse roles, from business lines operating across the world. Through this workshop they were able to begin to apply a shared standard for what the organization would say and do—no matter where and no matter what the business line.

We are ***driven, ingenious, and grounded****—relentlessly advancing the industry and our customer's businesses in surprising but practical ways.*

A simple and elegant definition of character can change everything. Providing a clear benchmark for what an organization—and each person inside—says and does.

8. Finalize

Once you've chosen your three essential character traits, draft a short statement that captures the words and ideas.

The core character statement need not be long. But include as much detail as necessary for others to understand the choices you've made.

You'll also find that walking employee groups through the process—using photos taken along the way—is an effective way to build support for the shared character definition. They will want to know the purpose of the work, who was involved, and whether their leadership supports the conclusions. It is also important to focus review sessions on the discussion of how the character, as defined, will affect their roles in the organization. Ask for their ideas and share the ideas of others.

Many organizations will have to consider how the traits translate into other languages. Work to capture the right meaning—not just to substitute equivalent words.

The brand character workshop will ignite a critical discussion within the organization—one that few companies ever have. It is a chance to air concerns about whether the organization is "losing what made it great" or "hanging onto a past that is no longer relevant." By opening up the topic, newcomers get a chance to add their views and old-timers get to retell the stories that have defined the culture.

The workshop does more than speed the process of defining the brand character. It ensures that people with differing views get a chance to arrive at an optimal solution together. That leads to actionable agreement.

A Workshop Alternative

Sometimes it's not possible to conduct workshops. Or you can reach some parts of your organization that way, but not all. A viable alternative is to interview people individually and in small groups using the past, present, future framework as a guide.

It's not hard to get people talking about the character of an organization, but you have to make them comfortable to get to what's true:

- Just as with the groups, explain why it is important to define character.
- Let them know that you're there to get their personal view.
- Make sure they understand what they say will be used, but without attribution. You'll only be identifying their general function or business unit—nothing that will reveal their identity.

Founders, CEOs, and other very senior leaders are an exception to this rule. Most will expect, even demand that their words be given the weight of their name and position. Follow their lead!

Begin by asking them to tell you stories that they think exemplify the character of the organization. Probe for why they chose specific traits. For example, if they feel that the organization was opportunistic in the past, ask for an example.

Don't be afraid to be provocative. Challenge the interviewee (politely) if you think they're just reading from the corporate script or being too cautious. Remind them that you need their personal view and that their identity is safe. Reassure them if they're concerned about having a different perspective than their peers.

Take good notes. Try to capture, verbatim, the most telling comments. It's often helpful to have a second person present to be the scribe so that you can concentrate on the conversation. Make sure you cover past, present, and emerging character traits.

Discuss the character of competitors. Ask, "What distinguishes their character?" and "How are we different?"

You can also review communications and marketing materials for clues to the organization's character. Is the tone serious or funny? Is the language sophisticated or straightforward? Are the images functional or expressive? Bring examples to the interviews to gauge whether or not people feel that the traits reflect the organization's character.

When you've completed the interviews, distill what you've learned, and with a small and trusted group, profile the past, present, and future—then winnow the traits down to the powerful three.

We used to be opportunistic—really had to be—now we're far more disciplined.

Customers don't need us to be nice; they need us to get it right the first time.

We were known as "the animals of Silicon Valley"—and proud of it!

Your notes have to capture the words and the ideas you're hearing in the interviews. To prove your case, you'll have to evoke the voices of the organization.

Arena

Where do you choose to compete? Who are your fiercest competitors? The arena provides the context and sets the standard for every competitive battle.

A Simple Question

What do you do? It's a simple question—one of the first we ask someone after being introduced. It's an important question because it provides a context for everything that follows—a conversation with an IRS Agent would be very different from one with a trapeze artist.

Choosing an arena is a first step in competing. It is a declaration of purpose. It sets the boundaries of what we do.

Arena is straightforward, but often overlooked. It is a statement of where the brand chooses to compete.

Defining your brand's competitive arena tells the world what you do and who your competitors are. It is the ring into which you have tossed your hat. A brand can't make the "long-list" of potential customers unless it tells its markets where it competes.

Defining arena can be challenging for diversified corporations.

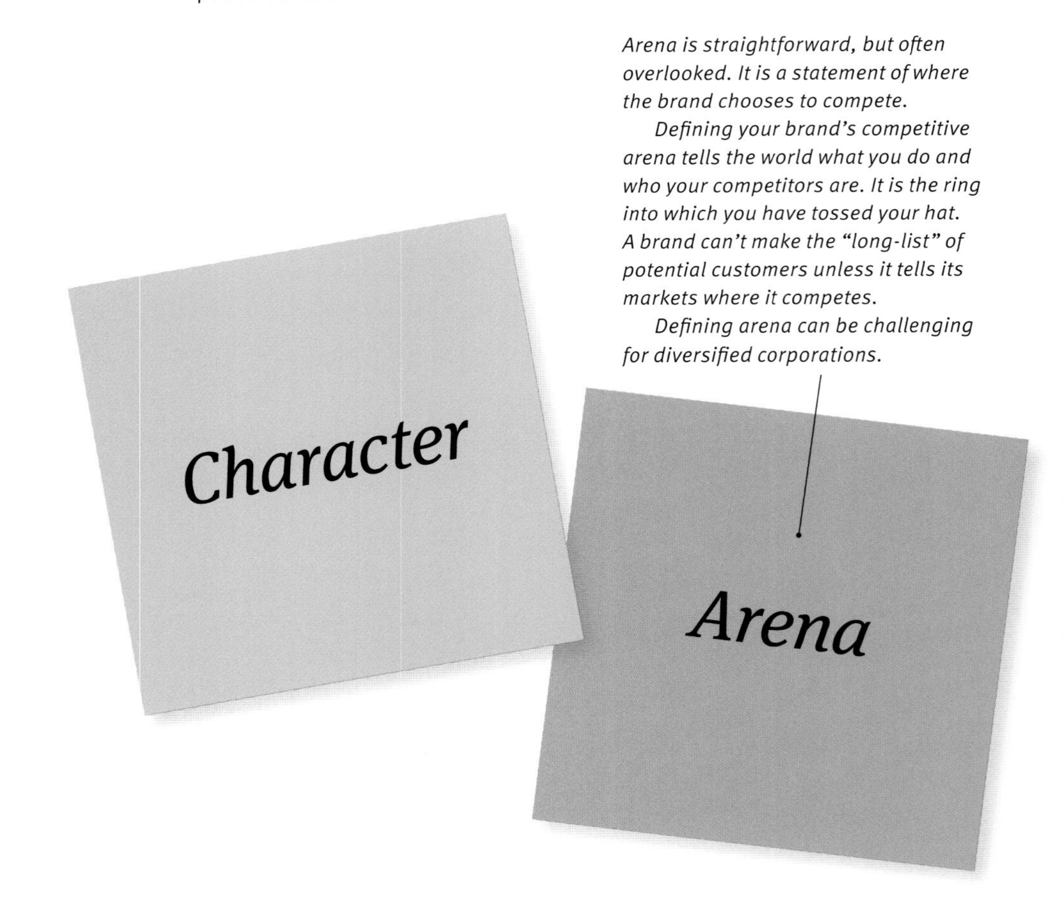

What do you do?

Positioning

Experience

Identity

Don't Use Your Imagination

Arenas should be generic. Their primary use is for context, for sorting. Don't get creative when declaring your arena. Why? Which is more useful, telling someone you are a "chromatic modulation technician" or a house painter?

One problem is that organizations aren't always satisfied with straightforward descriptors like, "Business Consulting," "Industrial Construction," or "Oil Field Services." They want to differentiate themselves from competitors. But arena is used to get on a prospect's radar, not to win the job.

If you want to be found, much less considered, your organization has to fit into the way prospects organize the world. If you need to build a gas-fired power plant, you'd search for "industrial construction" companies or "power plant construction."

Think of it this way. If you're searching for specific products and services you might ask a trusted friend, use the Yellow Pages (very retro), or Google prospective providers. You'll use generic terms no matter how you search. "I'm looking for... a butcher, a baker, a candlestick maker." When it comes to arena, separating yourself from the herd is not a good thing. You'll only be harder to find.

Define your arena in clear, simple, and generic terms. Don't use your imagination.

But what if there is no word or phrase that describes what you do? How can you describe something new, something that is truly innovative?

First, determine if you're really inventing a new industry. If you're just improving on what has been, there's no advantage in coining a new arena. Remember, you will have to teach people an entirely new idea. That's hard and expensive.

But, if you're sure you are pioneering a new industry, such as private space travel, you still can leverage what's come before.

Virgin Galactic describes its arena as "Commercial Spaceline." You can see how using a variant of "airline" allows them to coin a new arena name without confusion. But most important is their use of the word "space."

Woof-Proofer

Stray Rounder

Canine Controller

Dog Catcher

You may like some of these invented arena names, but only one is sure to get you on the long-list.

If you analyze the computer code behind their home page, you'll find over fifty instances of the word "space." It's there, over and over, because potential customers are going to be using that word as part of their search.

Another pitfall in defining an optimal arena is the tendency to "let the tail wag the dog." Arena tells prospective employees, customers, donors, investors, and others your chosen territory. While you want all of your products and services to fit inside, don't let outliers blur or distort your focus.

For example, if you're 99.99% a glass container maker, don't worry if you make a few plastic bottles or closures. Unless you plan on materially expanding the plastic side of your business, it need not be part of the lead descriptor of "what we do."

Caterpillar's lineage stretches back to 1904 when the Holt Manufacturing Company made the first Caterpillar tractor.

Caterpillar's arena grew from "Tractors" to "Earthmoving and Construction Equipment" to "Earthmoving and Construction Equipment and Services." But it didn't stop there.

Caterpillar added financial products, new services like logistics, and became a dominant generator-and engine-maker. Their competitive arena grew so expansive that it wasn't practical to just keep adding elements to the list. So they took a leap.

They redefined their chosen arena as "Enabling builders and planners." The advantage? Builders and planners would consider Caterpillar for new kinds of products and services.

Tractors

Earthmoving and Construction Equipment

Earthmoving and Construction Equipment and Services

Earthmoving, Construction, and Power

~~Equipment, Engines, and Logistics, Repair, and Financial Services~~

Enabling Builders and Planners

Focused Versus Expansive

One of the choices you will have to make in defining an organization's arena is focus versus expanse. The more focused your arena, the easier it is to explain and for people to remember. Caterpillar was once defined as a tractor company. Simple. Apple, computers. Their arenas were even part of their legal names.

But absolute focus isn't always possible or optimal. While it might start with a single product or service, many organizations become more diversified, more complex over time. There are advantages to choosing an arena with some room for growth and change—rather than having to teach the world about each stage of expansion.

The broader the arena, the larger the potential audience for your products and services.

Whatever your strategy, focus or expanse, you'll have to find a way to own that territory in the minds of your target audiences.

When it began, OXO® could have chosen to compete in the relatively narrow arena of "kitchen tools," but it targeted a far broader arena of "hand tools"— an arena where its philosophy of "universal design" could distinguish it from all others.

From a single potato peeler, OXO® has built a portfolio of over 750 Good Grips® hand tools.

Over the years OXO® has expanded its arena even further to include almost any household (or home office) item where universal design can make "everyday living easier."

Consider combining the arena workshop module with the others in this book. It's a good way to efficiently use the time of the assembled group.

It's possible to define arena without a workshop. Interview the range of people discussed earlier, do the prep work, and you should be able to find a strong solution.

As Easy as 1, 2, 3... 4

Defining brand arena isn't complicated. Conduct a workshop. You'll need participants who represent the full range of activities of the organization. It's also important to include people from different geographic regions—what's "standard" terminology may vary from state to state, country to country.

Involve business leaders, sales people, and marketing directors in this stage of the process. They know the marketplace and have the clout to decide what's best.

1. Prep

Good preparation will speed the process. Review your own and competitive websites, annual reports, capabilities brochures, industry analyst reports, and other easily available materials. Note the stock terms and phrases used to declare "what we do." In many instances there will be an obvious arena used by all.

Synthesize the prep information for the workshop participants. (And have them read this book!)

2. Define your audiences

It's not possible to define terms without knowing who you're talking to. "Modality Manager" may seem like gibberish to a layperson, but it is crystal clear to a hospital administrator.

Take the time to list and prioritize the key audiences for your brand. That likely includes prospective employees as well as customers, and may include regulators, shareholders, influencers, partners, and others. Once you know who is listening, you can evaluate what's most useful to them.

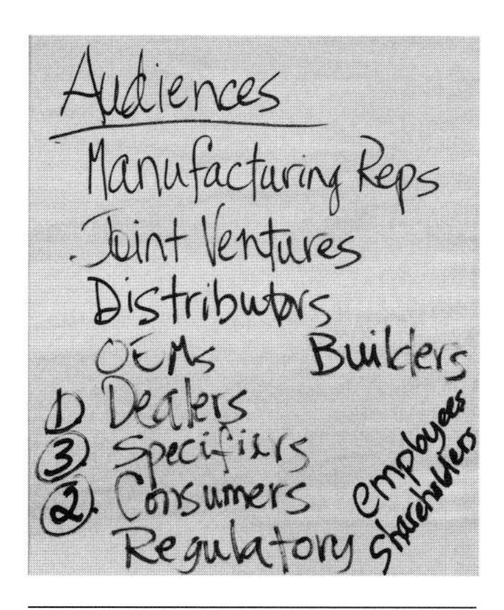

Define the key audiences that are part of your chosen arena. Prioritize those audiences.

3. List all the obvious alternatives

Write the standard terms and phrases onto a large pad or whiteboard. It's much easier to brainstorm when the raw materials are there for everyone to see.

4. Choose

Invest an hour in discussing the pros and cons of what's possible. If you're headed toward a laundry list of terms, see if there's a simple, encompassing term you can use instead.

Consider less obvious, but equally straightforward arenas. The brilliance of OXO® was in understanding that a universally superior "grip" was at the heart of their product and brand arena. They've built an iconic global brand on that simple insight.

Once you've exhausted the possibilities—choose. Again, this isn't about invention, it's about choice.

Positioning

Every arena has many players. Your competitiveness will be determined by the attributes that are associated with your brand. Choose and manage them carefully.

Brand Positioning

Brand positioning is exactly what it sounds like: how a brand stands in relation to its competitive brands.

For example, Geico is positioned as a low-cost, friendly alternative to more staid competitors. American Express distinguishes itself as a financial leader that always stands behind members. While these and other brands leverage their character to differentiate themselves, their offer is made even more distinctive and relevant through brand positioning.

Brand character is determined by a truth inside the organization, and arena is constrained by what is understood by key audiences—but positioning is driven by a mix of internal and external forces.

In this chapter, we will explore how to define the optimal positioning for a brand.

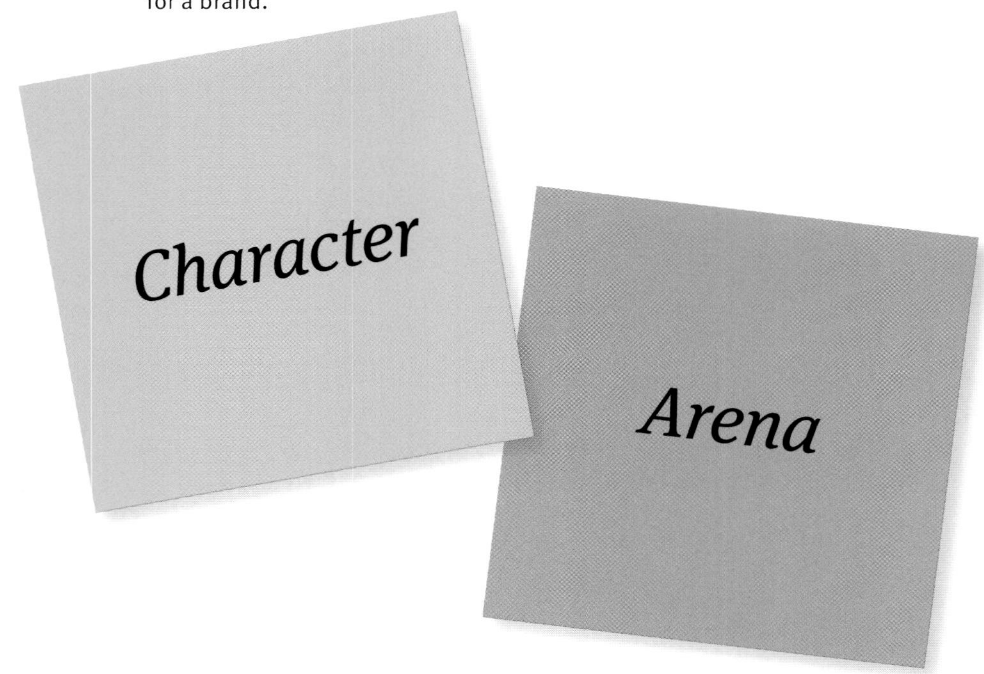

Getting short-listed requires communicating specific reasons (attributes) that are most important to a target audience.

Positioning gets tricky when you have diverse audiences who may have very different criteria for choice. "Drivers of choice" also change over time, which means that positioning must evolve as well.

Positioning

Experience

Identity

jetBlue®

McKinsey&Company

The Container Store®

The Original Storage and Organization Store®

Brand Territory—
A Simple Framework

When you think about a brand, what comes to mind? Is it the sheer scale and size of their operations? Is it a specific range of products and services? A way of doing things? The skills of the people behind the brand? Or perhaps, a clear purpose or mission?

Each of these territories—assets, offer, approach, skills , and mission—are archetypes that can be tapped to help us understand the fundamental nature of brands. While all brands touch on most of these territories, the best ones center on one or two.

Some territories are a more likely fit for some industries: approach- or skills-based for medical, legal, financial, and consulting services; asset- or product-based for industrial, wholesale, or leasing companies; mission for charities, government agencies, and political campaigns. But that's not always the case—or the best course.

3M started as a brand offering thousands of sticky and gritty products, but it is now positioned around its approach to "practical innovation." Avis relies on its vast assets—locations and fleets—to compete in the car rental business. But it positions itself on the approach, "We try harder." And Target has chosen to become known for its focus on design, not product range and cost. In fact, you can argue that less obvious and crowded positioning territories can be an advantage if you want to stand out. Unlike defining arena, a little imagination is an asset here.

All positioning territories are equally viable and equally valuable—the only consideration is which is the best fit and creates the greatest competitive advantage for an organization.

Keep in mind, positioning is not static. As organizations and markets evolve, so will the positioning of their brands.

If they've done their jobs well, you should be able to connect each of the brands at left to its chosen territory.

Assets

Offer

Approach

Skills

Mission

If you arrange the five territories in a continuum from tangible to intangible, you will have a simple but powerful framework for mapping brand positioning.

As you can see, a well-defined brand will have a center-of-gravity—even if it spills slightly over into an adjacent territory.

We think about The Home Depot® as always having a gigantic store, nearby, with everything a DIY'er might need. The Container Store® is, obviously, focused on containers. JetBlue® brings a unique attitude and approach to air travel. McKinsey & Company is renowned for the talents and skills they bring to every engagement. And the American Red Cross is unequivocally set on a mission.

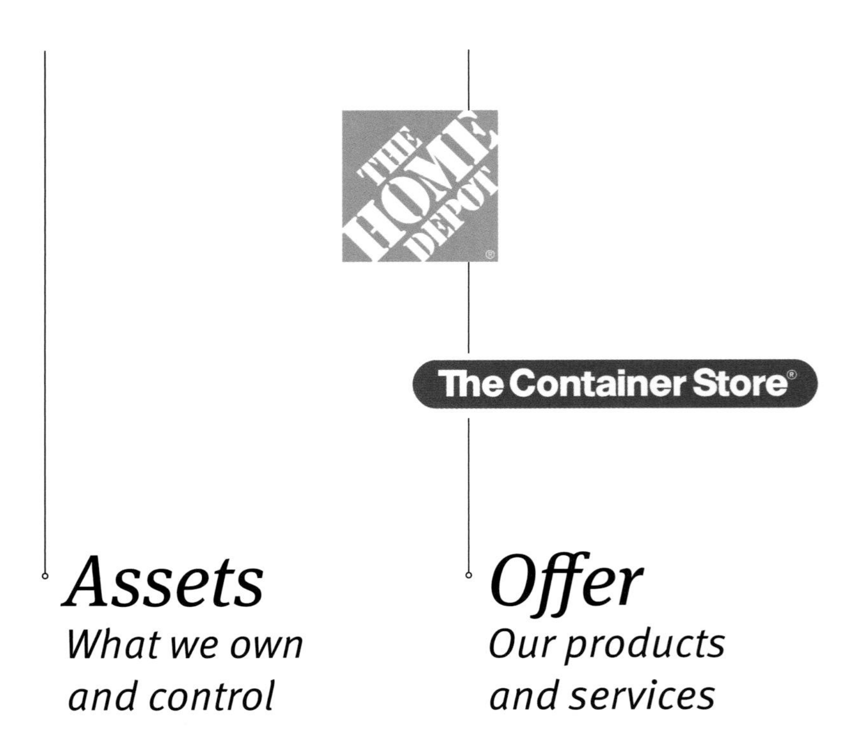

An organization positioned on assets does not have to operate without ideals. Nor does a company with a distinctive approach succeed without products and services. Positioning is "the pointy end of the spear." It is the clear and sharp point of differentiation that audiences you target will associate with the brand.

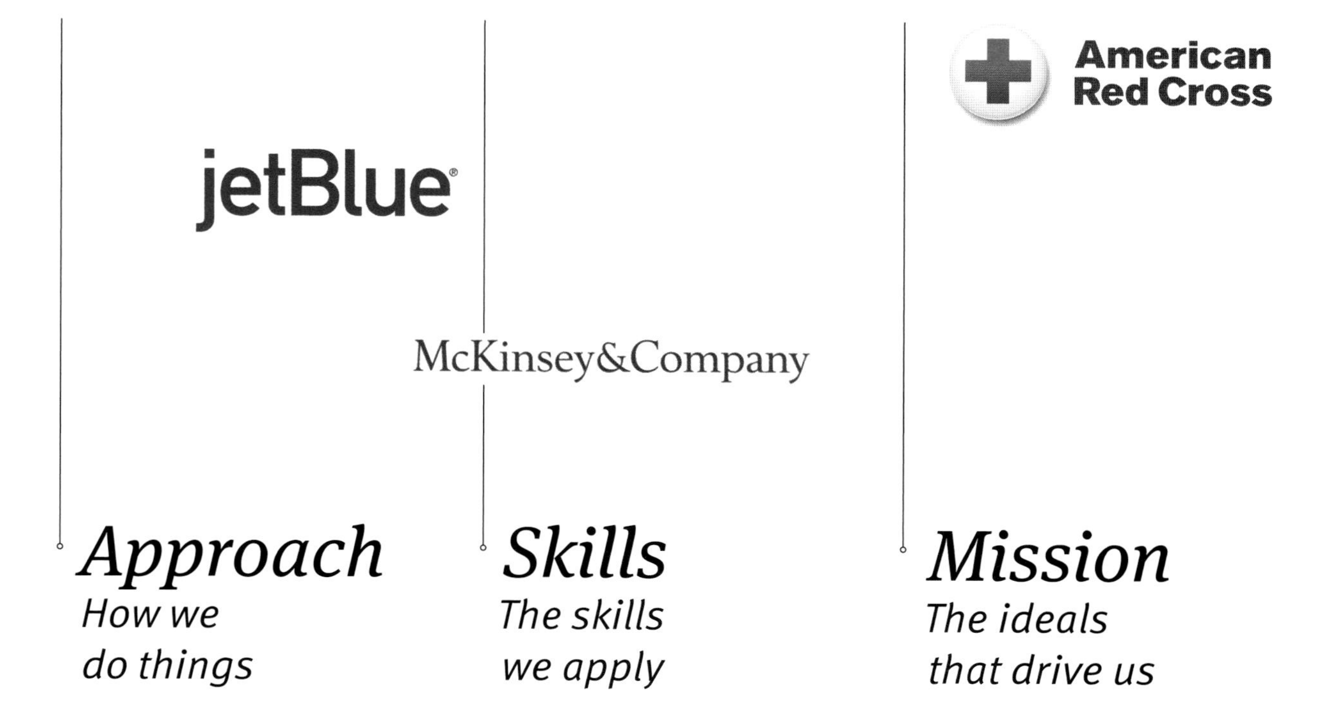

Successful brands take a stand; they have advocates and detractors.

It's possible to build a successful brand in any of the five territories. None is inherently superior to the other, but few, if any, organizations have what it takes to successfully compete in all five.

Here are five water brands that have staked out their own territory.

...sourced only from carefully selected springs...

Poland Springs

Assets

What we own and control

...a range of flavored waters with added vitamins and minerals.

Vitamin Water

Offer

Our products and services

Failures try to be everything to everyone, nobody cares very much about them.

Solutions for better water.™

Brita

Approach
How we do things

The World's Foremost Water Conditioning Expert Is In Your Neighborhood.™

Culligan

Skills
The skills we apply

Advocacy for improving the quality and supply of water in North America and beyond.

American Water Works Association

Mission
The ideals that drive us

Skills

Positioning Attributes

Positioning territories are big enough to hold many, many competitive brands. The differences are in the specific attributes that describe each one. For example, an asset-based positioning for a company might hinge on "an unmatched patent portfolio, private ownership, and seasoned employees" while another is touting the massive scale of its facilities, its deep financial resources, and serving the most Fortune 500™ customers. Both brands would have an asset-centered positioning, but no one would mistake one for the other.

Look carefully through the sample lists on the following spread. You'll notice that there are contradictory attributes, like "Good value" and "Premium," "Diverse" and "Specialized."

That's because the attribute lists represent what might be important to a range of customers, employees, partners, investors, and other key audiences. Unfortunately, not all audiences are swayed by the same attributes and sometimes they have conflicting requirements.

Make sure your lists include all of the attributes that might be claimed by every potential provider. For example, if you were seeking a financial advisor, you would research the offers of a number of providers. One might claim superior results through a "proprietary process," another the backing of a "large research department," and a third that they only represent "ethical and green" investments. All of those attributes would go into a comprehensive territory map of the industry.

A positioning map populated by every important attribute for an arena is a critical starting point for defining a positioning for any brand.

Years in business
Market cap
Number of employees
Number of locations
Fleet
Patents
Reviews, testimonials, awards
Number of clients/customers
Technical infrastructure
Public company
Private company
Certifications
Large scale
Tenure of employees
Client retention
Redundancy
Network of suppliers
Network of distributors
Low-cost structure
World-class facilities

Assets

What we own and control

Range of products/services
Focus of products/services
Reliable products/services
Good value
Cheap
Premium
Limited editions
Size variations
Flavor variations
Packaging variations
Look and feel
Smell
Sound
Portability
Bulk
Tailored to age
Tailored to lifestyle

Offer

Our products and services

These are examples of the kind of attributes that might fit into the five territories.

Collaborative
Treats you like a partner
Flexible
Relentless
Right the first time
Culturally sensitive
"Green"
Rapid prototyping
Cautious, bulletproof
Overbuilt
Clear chain of command
Collegial
US-based
Multinational
Global
Tight quality controls
Encourages experimentation
Constantly evolving
Straightforward, simple
Can quickly scale operations

Approach

How we do things

Industry expertise
Highly credentialed
Continued training
Cross-disciplined
Diverse
Specialized
Renowned staff
Relates well to leadership
Able to engage the entire organization
Great leaders
Fast learners
Proven/certified/licensed
Rare
Unique

Skills

The skills we apply

Improve...
Advocate...
Advance...
End...
Enable...
Fight...
Defend...
Preserve...
Take back...
Recast...

Mission

The ideals that drive us

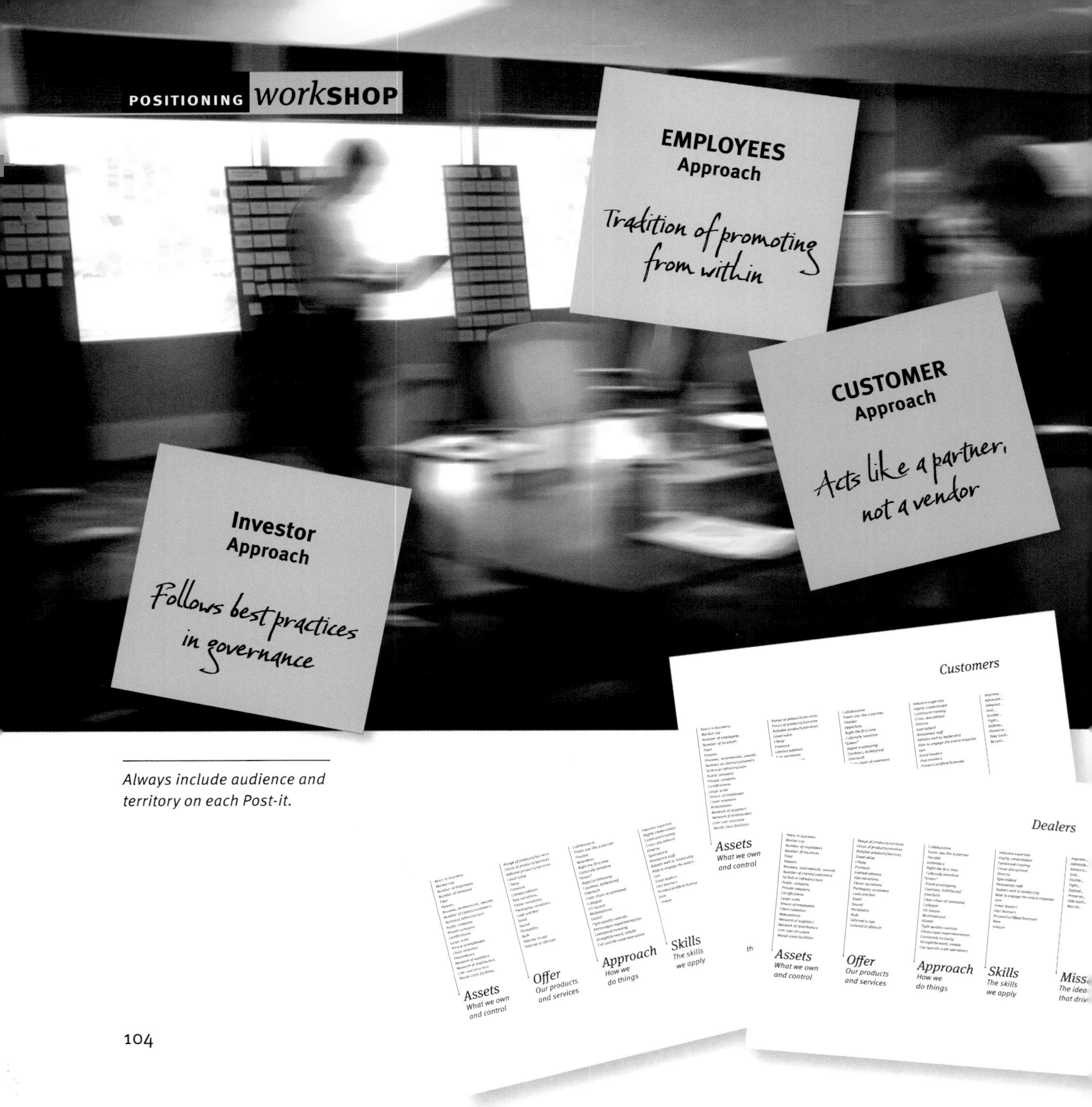

Always include audience and territory on each Post-it.

1. Prep

Using the audience journeys, interviews, research reports, and strategic plans from the discovery phase, identify messages, ideas, and experiences (broken into attributes) to populate the appropriate positioning territories.

This is easier than you might imagine. Simply collect and sort the attributes that emerge—using the topics listed on pages 102–103 as a guide. Remember, you are deriving those attributes from the perspective of each audience, not limiting them to ones touted by one organization. You want to capture all of the primary attributes that are part of the arena.

Generalize the attributes. If you read "100 years in business," translate that into "a pioneer in the industry" or "very long industry tenure." A list of every product type imaginable would become "a comprehensive array of products." "Close coordination of our five business units" would simply become "close coordination across business units."

Prepare a positioning attribute sheet for each audience. This will allow you to assess the similarities and differences in what drives choice for each audience in your chosen arena.

As shown at left, create arrays of Post-its, printed with single attributes and organized into assets, offer, approach, skills, and mission territories. Include the audience and territory on each one. You can even color-code them by audience. It is easiest to arrange them on large foam-core boards in advance of the workshop, but you can just use a long wall or window to set up the exercise.

Create a positioning attribute sheet for each audience. There may be considerable duplication of attributes from audience to audience. That's to be expected.

American
Red Cross

2. Frame

Take advantage of the examples and frameworks in this chapter to bring the work group up to speed. Positioning is one of the most complex areas of brand definition, but it is a close cousin to business strategy development. In organizations that are skeptical about the value of "soft" disciplines like branding, this exercise is an eye-opener.

It also helps to have tapped into key members of the group in the prep work. They will have a stake in the outcome of the workshop and can help their peers with the process.

"Once the group understood the strategic implications of what we were doing, they began to see branding in a new light."

Draw on the examples in this book to provide context for the positioning workshop.

Infrastructure
Superior returns
Consistency of performance

3. Brainstorm

Even with extensive pre-workshop prep, the group will need to add to the arrays of attributes in each of the positioning territories. Let them review and discuss what's already there, then jump into brainstorming to determine what's missing.

It's important that every strong attribute is surfaced. Remind the group that customers and other audiences will consider all competitors in the arena for what they want and need—so they should not limit attributes to the ones that they believe their organization can deliver.

The brainstorming session is an ideal time to push the boundaries of potential attributes. The starting lists are based primarily on what has been. But the leaders of the future may bring innovations that overturn old ways. Ask the group to consider adding new ideas to the mix that they believe could advance the industry.

This work should take about an hour. Encourage and push the group until they lose steam.

When they're done, the arrays of Post-its will seem quite daunting: clearly too many ideas to be actionable. Don't worry, the next steps will provide a framework and method to get to only the attributes that really matter.

Give the group a short break before moving on to the next step—P.I.E.

The group should add a number of attributes to the pre-prepared arrays—filling in any gaps in the pre-workshop arrays. Encourage the group to consider ideas that have not traditionally been applied to their arena.

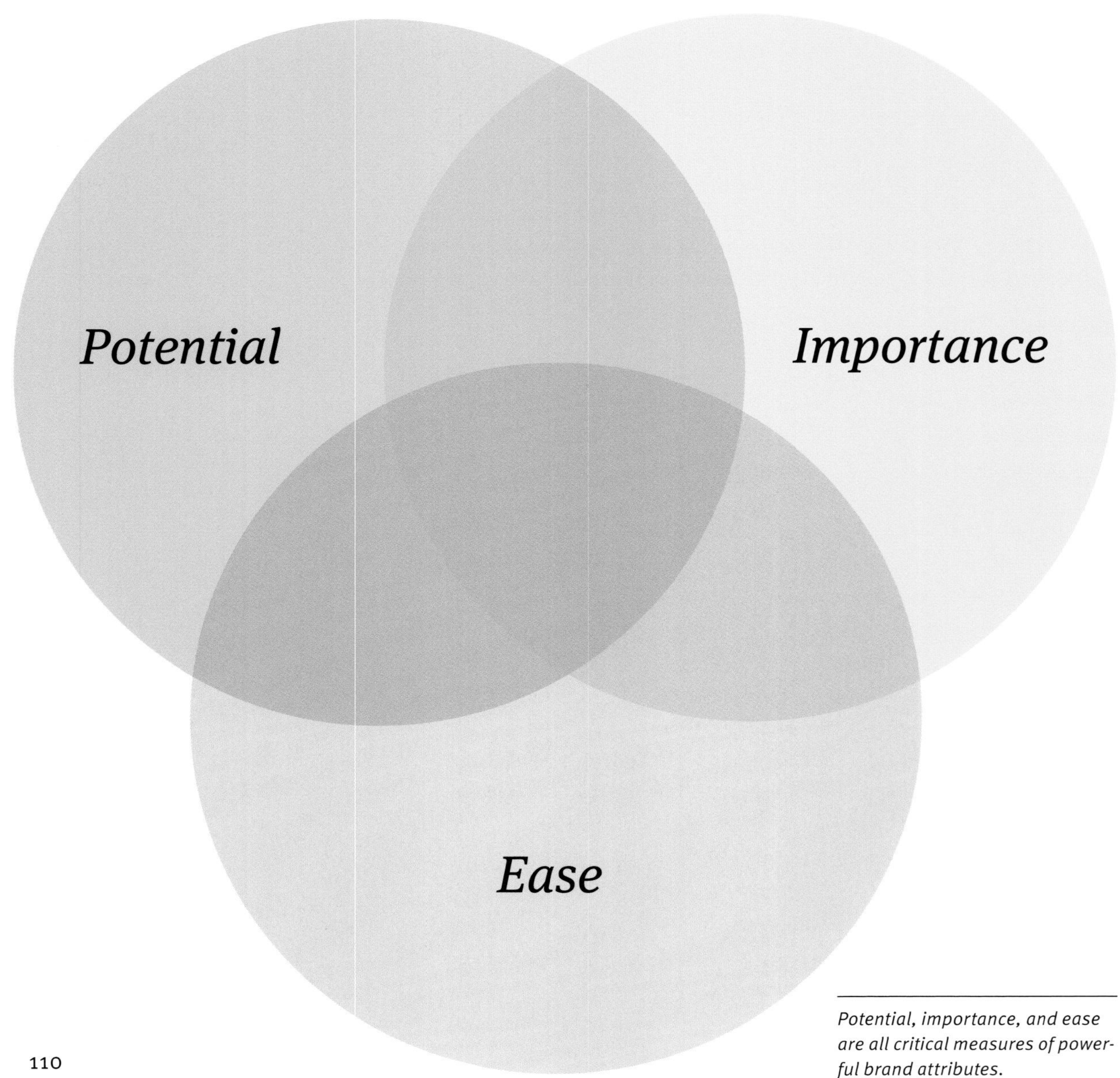

Potential, importance, and ease are all critical measures of powerful brand attributes.

4. P.I.E.

Long lists of attributes are not that useful. While they give you a sense of what's part of the arena, you'll need to identify the most powerful attributes to gain real competitive advantage. There are three dimensions that define an ideal attribute: potential, importance, and ease. P.I.E.

Potential is the relative leverage of one attribute versus another to drive choice among your key audiences. Does improving a brand's high rating on "puts my interests first" win more business than "locations near me?" Or does becoming known for "cheapest products in the marketplace" deliver the biggest payoff for the effort?

Unfortunately, improving the rating on some attributes may gain you nothing. If you already are seen as having locations that are close enough, telling me you're adding more is a waste of resources.

You want to choose attributes with the highest potential to move minds and markets. Go for the most bang for the buck.

Importance, or correlation with choice, is a ranking of the attributes that influence choice from most to least. Look at the top 10 and you'll get a good sense of why an arena's leading brands are winning today.

Ease is a combination of factors. Cost is one. Is it expensive to improve your rating on an attribute? Again, if you want to rate best on "location near you," it might require a massive real estate effort. Not easy.

Ease is also a measure of how an attribute fits your character. Even if "collaborates well" is important and has great potential to win customers, if your character is more "cowboy" than "caring," it won't be easy.

Finally, ease is a measure of "permission." Will key audiences believe it's possible for you to deliver? If Wal-Mart said it was going to become a luxury goods store you'd scoff. It wouldn't matter if they meant it; getting you to accept such a change would not be easy.

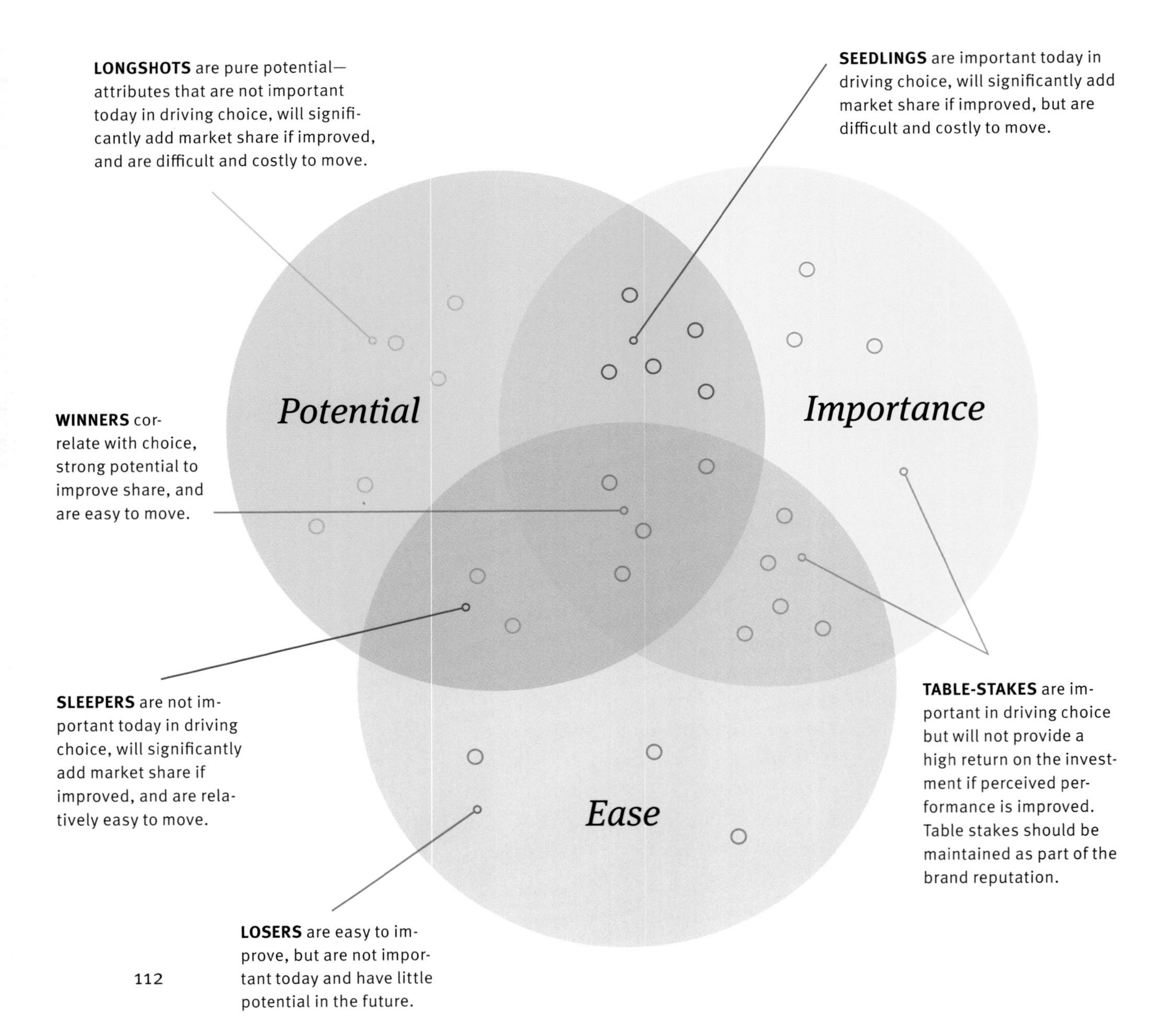
LONGSHOTS are pure potential—attributes that are not important today in driving choice, will significantly add market share if improved, and are difficult and costly to move.
SEEDLINGS are important today in driving choice, will significantly add market share if improved, but are difficult and costly to move.
Potential
Importance
WINNERS correlate with choice, strong potential to improve share, and are easy to move.
SLEEPERS are not important today in driving choice, will significantly add market share if improved, and are relatively easy to move.
TABLE-STAKES are important in driving choice but will not provide a high return on the investment if perceived performance is improved. Table stakes should be maintained as part of the brand reputation.
Ease
LOSERS are easy to improve, but are not important today and have little potential in the future.

The workshop group will evaluate the long attribute list to identify ones that have the greatest potential, importance, and ease. They'll need to rely on their experience and the intelligence gathered during the audit phase.

A few attributes will have high potential, importance, and ease. Many will rate highly on only one or two dimensions. Some will fit none and should be discarded.

Distribute the attributes in the diagram—those that deliver all three dimensions go into the overlap in the center. Others will fit into one, or into the overlap between two dimensions. Step back. Take a close look at these three zones.

Winners, the attributes at dead center, are extremely valuable brand building blocks. They are already important to choice, have the potential to win more market share if improved, and are relatively easy to implement.

Sleepers are a bit like wild cards. They are new ideas, innovations, or something that everyone does, but not well. They are not "important" to the market today—only because they haven't yet been introduced to the market or nobody has figured out how to implement them properly. That's what makes them potentially groundbreaking.

Table-stakes are attributes that you have to deliver on to even compete in the arena but don't differentiate one brand from the next—like "a fleet of airplanes" for airlines. You won't defeat competitors with table-stakes.

These are key zones for positioning attributes, but don't ignore **Longshots**, **Seedlings**, and **Losers**. There is something to learn from them all.

Divide the workshop group into teams that represent key audiences. Their task is to evaluate each attribute. Does it have high potential, importance, or ease for their audience? They can tap into their own experience as well as data from the audit to make those judgments.

If you consolidate the separate audience diagrams into one brand-wide view you can see which attributes are most relevant and useful across the board.

Some organizations use the workshops to finalize potential attribute lists and conduct a preliminary, qualitative evaluation with attendees. They then field quantitative research to assess, with certainty, the potential, importance, and ease (permission) of the attribute array.

Here, the group (my Masters of Professional Studies Branding class at the School of Visual Arts) is profiling four audiences. They will then be consolidated into a single brandwide diagram.

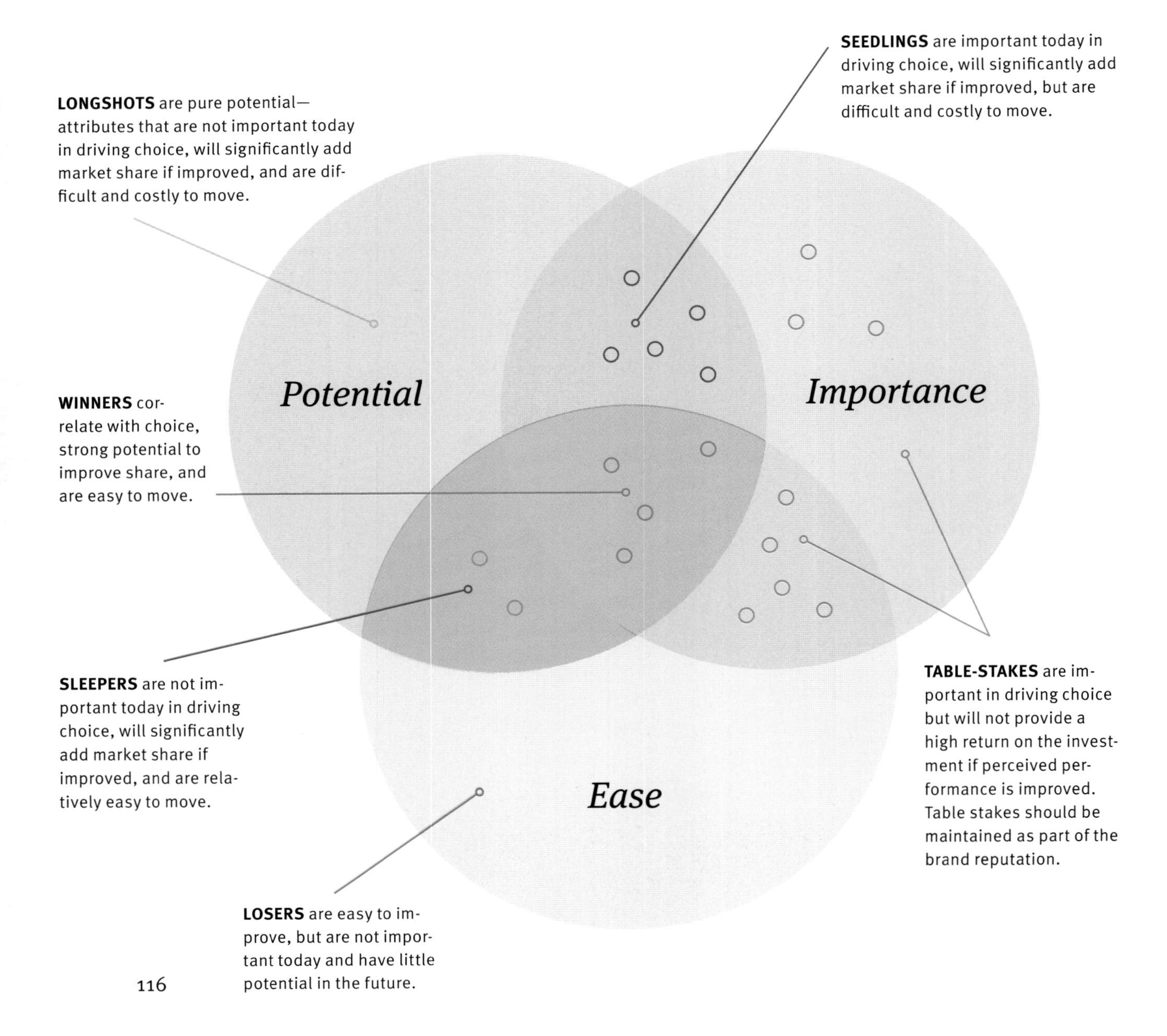

SEEDLINGS are important today in driving choice, will significantly add market share if improved, but are difficult and costly to move.
LONGSHOTS are pure potential—attributes that are not important today in driving choice, will significantly add market share if improved, and are difficult and costly to move.
Potential
Importance
WINNERS correlate with choice, strong potential to improve share, and are easy to move.
SLEEPERS are not important today in driving choice, will significantly add market share if improved, and are relatively easy to move.
Ease
TABLE-STAKES are important in driving choice but will not provide a high return on the investment if perceived performance is improved. Table stakes should be maintained as part of the brand reputation.
LOSERS are easy to improve, but are not important today and have little potential in the future.

5. Distill

Once you've plotted each attribute on the "map," focus in on the Winners at the center and the Sleepers at the intersection of Potential and Ease. Together, these represent the attributes with the greatest likelihood and power to drive choice.

If you want to consider attributes with a less immediate payoff, but long-term value, look at Seedlings. They're worth considering, but won't be easy to make a part of the brand's meaning.

When you pull out these most powerful attributes, you've distilled the essence of what's relevant to key audiences and within reach for the organization.

Don't forget to note all of the attributes in the Importance circle. You won't win the market with them, but you must maintain reasonable performance for most, or you won't even get a chance to compete.

Don't expect many attributes to pass through the P.I.E. filter. In fact, you're best off with a handful. Fewer elements will make it easier to focus the brand positioning.

When distilling down to the most powerful attributes, concentrate on Winners that have potential, importance, and ease, and Sleepers, attributes that represent new ideas that are practical to develop and have the potential to change the industry.

At minimum, plan on maintaining attributes with Importance. They are the cost of entry that every competitor must pay.

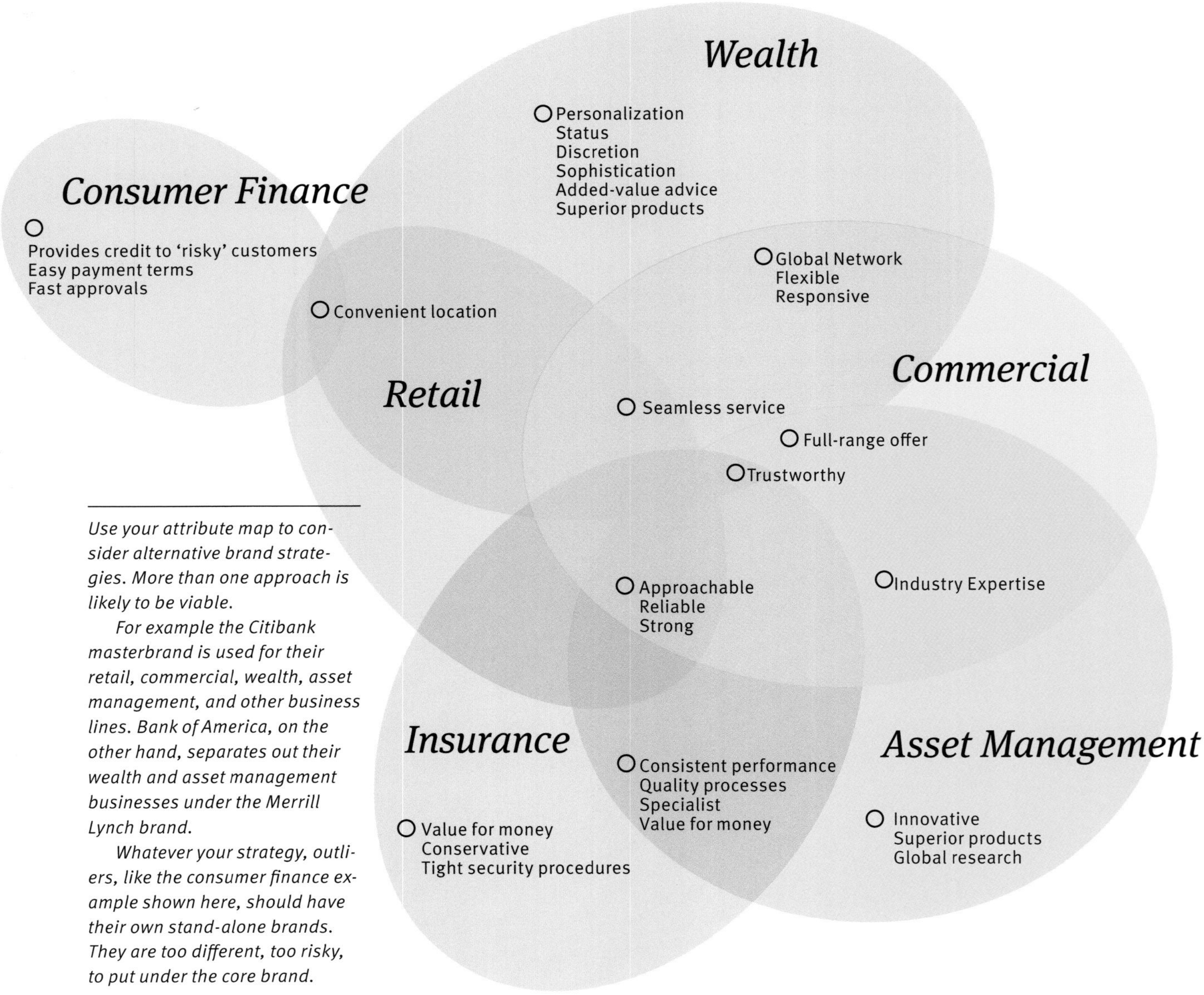

Wealth

Personalization
Status
Discretion
Sophistication
Added-value advice
Superior products

Consumer Finance

Provides credit to 'risky' customers
Easy payment terms
Fast approvals

Global Network
Flexible
Responsive

Convenient location

Commercial

Retail

Seamless service

Full-range offer

Trustworthy

Approachable
Reliable
Strong

Industry Expertise

Insurance

Asset Management

Consistent performance
Quality processes
Specialist
Value for money

Value for money
Conservative
Tight security procedures

Innovative
Superior products
Global research

Use your attribute map to consider alternative brand strategies. More than one approach is likely to be viable.

For example the Citibank masterbrand is used for their retail, commercial, wealth, asset management, and other business lines. Bank of America, on the other hand, separates out their wealth and asset management businesses under the Merrill Lynch brand.

Whatever your strategy, outliers, like the consumer finance example shown here, should have their own stand-alone brands. They are too different, too risky, to put under the core brand.

Some organizations have such diversity in their businesses that there are legitimate questions as to whether they should operate under a single "masterbrand."

One way to determine the optimal relationship of the parts to the whole (brand architecture) is to map the intersection of the attributes that are optimal for each of the primary business lines. Think of this as a double-distilled view.

Construct a diagram, like the one at left, that maps the key drivers of choice for each business line and where they overlap.

A financial services organization with retail, wealth, commercial, wholesale, and insurance business lines might find that its investment-oriented businesses need to emphasis service and performance attributes, while its savings and insurance businesses must project safety and stability.

Once you've 'populated' a diagram it should become clearer if, where, and how the business lines share key drivers of choice.

Organizations with many business lines have to weigh the advantages of a strong, unified "masterbrand" for all (or most) against the focus created by multiple brands.

Business lines that share a strong core of attributes can share the same brand. A business line that overlaps partially might be best only "endorsed" by the parent brand. A business that seeks customers with entirely different priorities may need its own brand.

Partnership

Is flexible.
Acts as a partner, not a vendor.
Drives demand for products

Innovation

Accelerates progress.
Drives innovation.
Is at the forefront with leading technology.
Has superior products.

Dependability

Always meets your needs.
Is dependable.

Experience

Offers technical advice when you need it.
Has knowledgeable people.
Understands the industry.

6. Craft

A carefully considered list of relevant and powerful attributes isn't enough. They have to be relevant to all of your most important audiences, make sense as a set, and suggest coherent themes.

If you've done a good job of evaluating the attributes for fit with the brand character (as part of Ease) you will find that they fit perfectly with who you are, not just what you do.

You'll need to work with the attributes here, just as you did with the character traits. Not to reduce them to three—but to make sure that the ones you select reinforce each other to create a whole that's bigger than its parts. Craft an idea out of the elements.

Brand positioning is not absolute. There can be more than one valid and effective stance for a brand. Just build your ideas from the right elements.

The arena, character, and attribute work will give you a highly focused palette of elements to consider before finalizing a working brand positioning.

Avoid the pitfall of trying to create a totally unique positioning. Fitting into an arena is just as important as standing out. You goal is to win and retain the support of key audiences far more often.

These attributes were distilled using P.I.E. They represent strong positioning elements, but a list is not enough. When clustered, strong themes like partnership, innovation, dependability, and experience emerge. Think of these as potential positioning building blocks, and along with character and arena, as the essential elements of a better brand.

Kompetenz und Verantwortung
Changing the World with Great Care®

"Since we introduced aspirin over 100 years ago, Bayer has been dedicated to changing the world with great care."

7. Articulate

Finding just the right way to express an idea takes time and dedication. But when it's just right, you will have a powerful tool to advance new ideas that will redefine the organization. The workshop is a good place to explore possibilities—preliminary articulations that can be honed later.

One example of this process is the development of a brand positioning for Bayer in the U.S. The German-based multinational had lost control of the Bayer brand as part of reparations following WWI. That's why Americans pronounce it as "bear," not "buy-er," and think all the company does is make aspirin.

The non-U.S. parts of Bayer all operate under the brand positioning of "Kompetenz und Verantwortung" (Expertise with Responsibility). The defining attributes of a mission to improve the world through pharmaceuticals, health technologies, animal care, agriculture, and more are common to Bayer's businesses, including those in the USA. Also shared is a culture of immense discipline and care in the development and introduction of new products.

But the articulation of the positioning had to be appropriate to U.S. audiences. That's why "Changing the World With Great Care" was born. Its meaning is very close to the German expression, but it's not a straight translation. Bayer recognized that it had to rethink the wording to make its unique culture and mission understandable and accessible in America.

The goal is to articulate a simple and elegant statement that captures a differentiating competitive positioning, as well as the unique character of the organization.

Bayer could have simply translated its global positioning for use in the U.S. marketplace. Instead, it recast the idea of "Expertise with Responsibility" into a positioning statement that captured the character and attributes of the company in a way that would be relevant to American audiences.

POSITIONING
*work*SHOP

1. Prep
2. Frame
3. Brainstorm
4. P.I.E.
5. Distill + Distill
6. Craft
7. Articulate

Short films are a great way to communicate a new brand positioning. Even a rough cut with a simple voice over and music can help bring the brand idea to life.

The rough can be refined as the brand is further developed—providing a great tool to introduce the new brand program in- and outside of the organization.

PLAN
CUSTOMIZE
WARNING
RECOVER
FOUNDED
1989
BRIGHTPOINT

OLIVIA
VERNA
SPIDE
OY

Experience

Unlike the barker at the sideshow, brand stewards must deliver on their promises if they want their customers to return—to build loyalty.

Experience Is Undeniable

Some people think of branding as a ruse, a manipulation. And it can be. "Poser" brands lure us in and then fail to deliver. They are compelling, but not true. That's a viable strategy for businesses with little conscience, an economic model that does not rely on retaining customers, and has no need for a substantive reputation to "close the sale."

But for most organizations, their brands must be compelling and true to thrive. The experience they deliver should match—and preferably exceed—the promises they've made.

In this chapter, we will explore how to model the ideal experience based on how you've defined your brand. That model can then guide the planning and development of the brand in the real world.

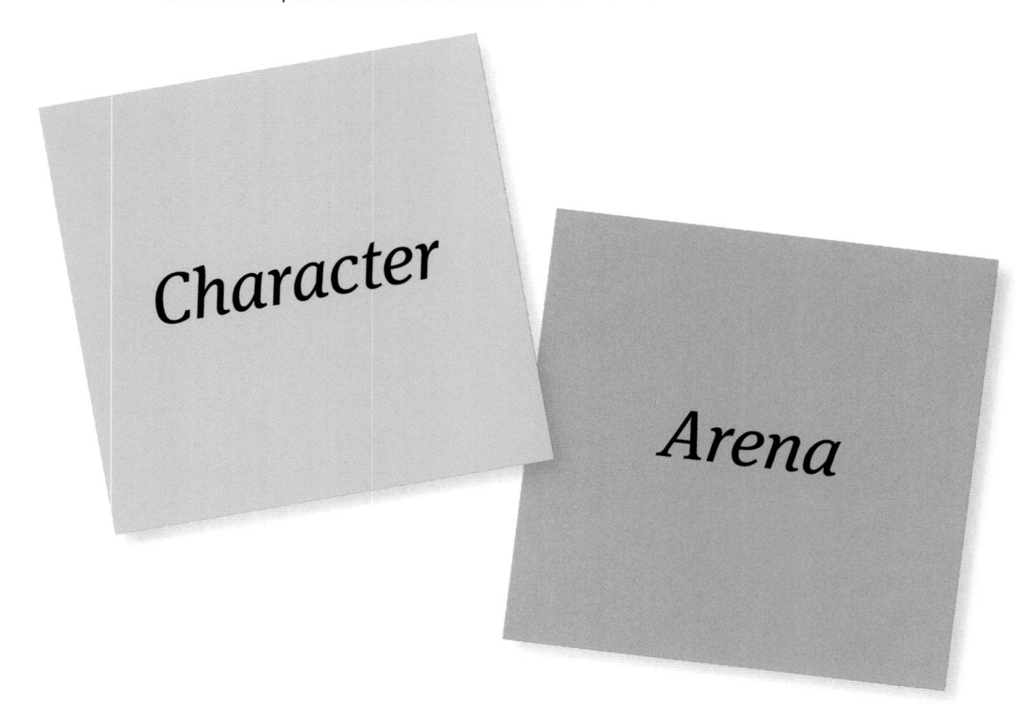

A consistent failure to deliver on a brand's promise will lead to its demise. That's why thinking through every aspect of the brand experience is so important.

Great brands develop and test comprehensive models of their brand experience—listening carefully to the feedback of key audiences. They then re-engineer their operations, train their employees and partners, and evolve the real-world brand experience.

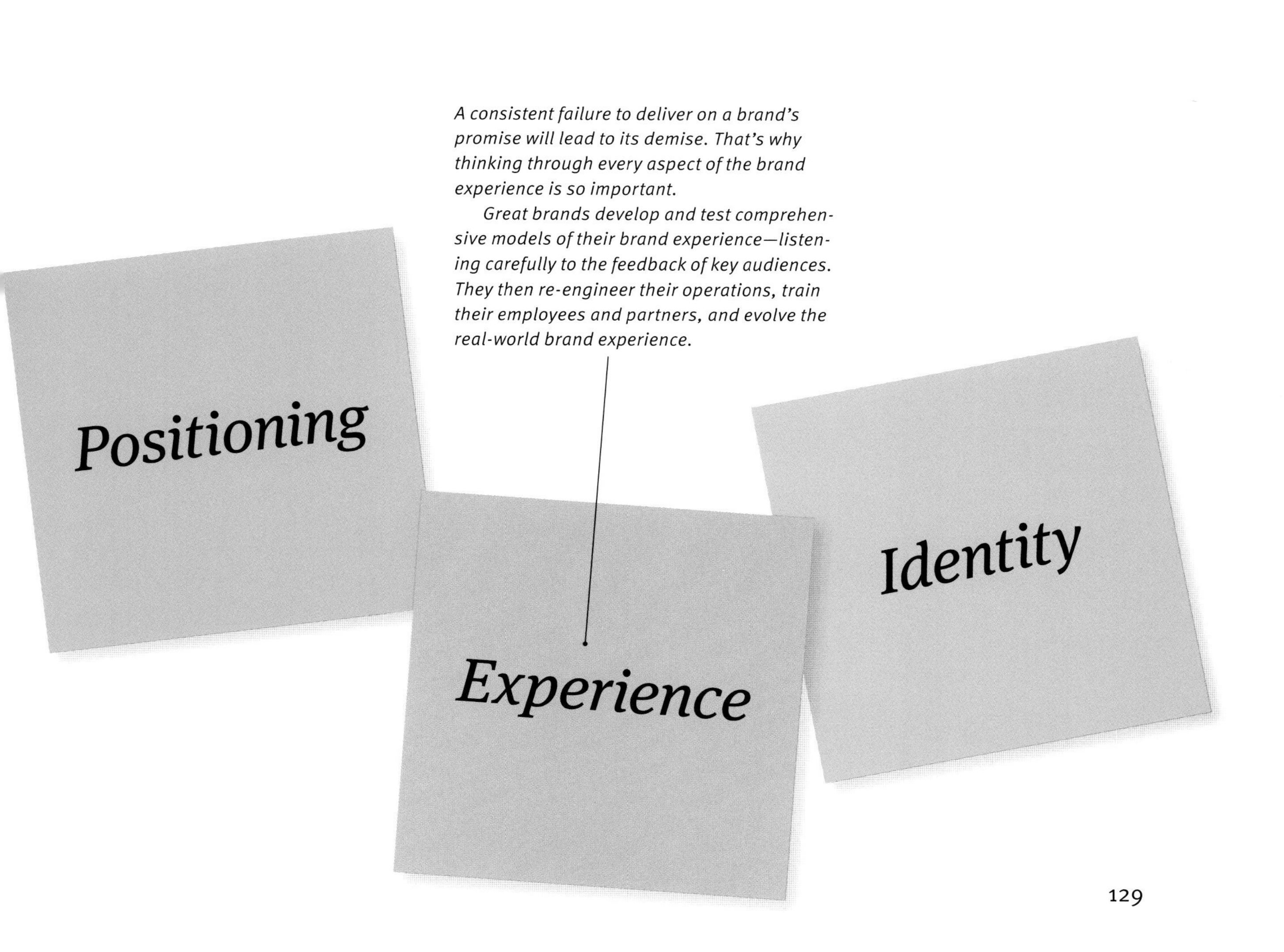

ANYTHING IS POSSIBLE IN A SKETCH!

(re)Model the Experience

Models have been used as a way to explore possibilities, work out technical problems, and gauge and gain support for complex and expensive projects. Models are particularly important when the endeavor is controversial, innovative, ambitious, or all three.

When you model a brand program, you are examining the journey, the entire experience of key audiences. You need to simulate what they see, hear, feel, and smell as they learn, choose, interact, and bond with your brand.

Use your "brand journey" work from the discovery phase as a basis for remodeling the experience.

One of the advantages of modeling is that you can vary the level of realism and depth. A sketch might be more than enough in some instances; a small mock-up perfect for others.

Start Stop Continue

1. Recast the Journey

One of the most effective approaches to recasting the brand journey is to gather a diverse group of people from across the organization for a brand experience workshop.

Take the group through the brand arena, character, and positioning work. Review the audience journeys you developed in the discovery phase. Then begin brainstorming how to recast the experience.

What fits and what needs to change? Are there new ideas for how and what the organization can do? Where will audiences feel you've kept (or broken) the new brand promise? Use words and sketches to capture ideas.

Essentially, the organization has to decide what it will start, stop, and continue to do to create a compelling experience that is true to its brand.

The Washington Center (TWC) is the premier center for academic internships in Washington and beyond. As part of an ambitious 5-year plan, they examined every aspect of their mission, methods, and marketing.

Here, TWC staffers discuss how the experiences of their students, employer partners, affiliate schools, donors, and others should change.

Learn
Choose
Interact
Bond

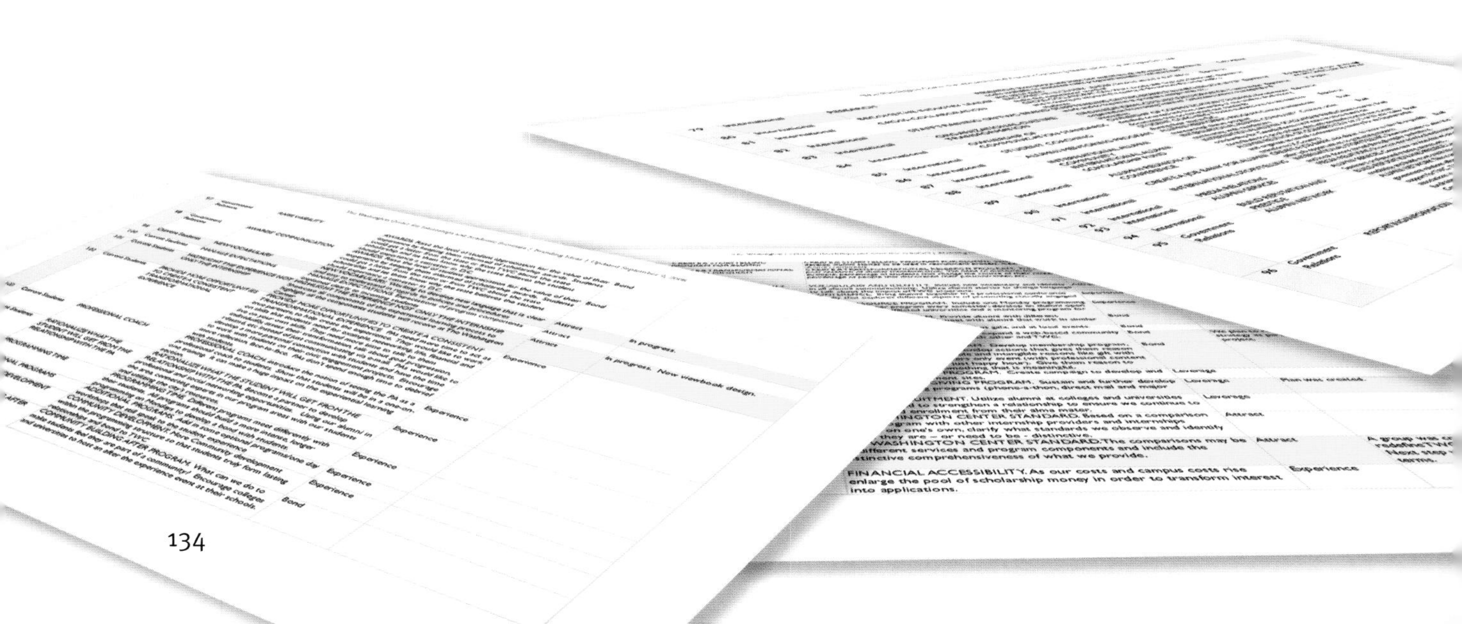

2. Prioritize Ideas

The workshop will generate ideas for aligning and improving the brand experience that should be collected and organized by audience and the stage (learn, choose, interact, or bond).

You're likely to have far too many ideas to implement at once. To prioritize, look at the workshop findings for each audience.

You may find that some audiences are in relatively good shape and only need a few, well-chosen changes. Others may be in dire straits. For example, we often find that an organization may be great in the "learn" and "choose" stages, but is poor at providing follow-on services and communications. Others do well with building loyalty, but have little depth in customer acquisition.

Cost and ease should also be considered. Many of the ideas could be put immediately into practice. But some may require months, even years, of effort and investment to truly deliver.

The ideas you select as high priority—short, medium, and long-term—will form the basis for the next step: modeling the future.

The Washington Center developed literally hundreds of potential ideas to improve their services and brand experience.

Those ideas were prioritized and translated into work plans that outlined specific timing, costs, and responsibilities.

EXPERIENCE

*work*SHOP

1. Recast the journey
2. Prioritize ideas
3. Model the future
4. Test
5. Embed

A View of the Future
ECONOMICS
PERFORMANCE
DEMAND
DEMAND INDEX
TOUCH
www.invista.com/flooring
Carol R. Gee
Global Director, Brands
INVISTA™
Built on DuPont Innovation
Invista Inc.
CRP 722 - Walnut Run
4417 Lancaster Pike, Room 206
Wilmington DE, 19880-0722
302-999-3971 tel
carol.r.gee@invista.com
www.invista.com/designermolecule

3. Model the Future

Translating ideas into expression and action isn't easy. It takes specialized experience and talent. Much like the research methods described earlier, you may need specialized help.

But even if you're not a trained marketer, designer, writer, organizational guru, or process engineer, you can oversee and guide the process. In fact, fostering the collaboration of the organization and disparate creative and strategic talent is what separates mediocre from magnificent brand programs.

DuPont's decision to spin-off its synthetic fibers businesses put a high-stakes process into motion. The challenge? Merge $6.2 billion worth of businesses into a cohesive new entity and brand. That meant creating a strategic brand positioning for what would be the world's largest stand-alone integrated synthetic fibers business, creating a new name and identity, and developing an actionable model of how the newborn giant would look, sound, and act. Even before it had its new name, "INVISTA," the organization had modeled how it would tell its story—from beginning to end—from one end of the world to the other.

Modeling the future of the brand is not logo development. While identity development can be a folded into the process (see the next chapter), its purpose is to explore how the organization might change everything for the better.

You have to keep in mind that you're planning a complete journey, not a series of disparate events. Consider what happens over a period of time. What is the short-, medium-, and long-term impression created by the organization? How can the brand project a powerful and coherent voice wherever it lives?

Consider more than surface changes. Be bold. Reorganize divisions, acquire companies, hire new talent, and shed outdated ideas and product lines.

Remember, this is a risk-free simulation of what could be.

Explore more than one path forward. Take the opportunity to broaden the possibilities. Don't reject outliers. All you need are talent and pencils to bring the ideas to life. Capture the spirit of ideas. Quickly.

Create a series of examples that illustrate the journey of each key audience. Review and refine with leadership and key parts of the organization. Tie the examples back to their strategic underpinnings.

Once you've thoroughly explored what's possible, you're ready for the next step: concept testing.

Modeling the future of a brand is a bit like creating a stage set that's complete enough to tell a convincing story.

EXPERIENCE

*work*SHOP

1. Recast the journey
2. Prioritize ideas
3. Model the future
4. Test
5. Embed

4. Test

You now have everything you need to test a new brand model for the future.

1. You've defined the arena, character, and positioning of the brand, so you know, overall, what has to be communicated by everything the organization does.

2. Since your positioning idea is built on discrete attributes, you have the ideal basis for designing meaningful and effective quantitative research.

3. The model of the customer's—and other audiences'—experience can be used in testing to gauge the clarity, relevance, distinctiveness, credibility, and the ability to positively affect behavior (like buy your products, work for you, invest, etc.). There's nothing better than clear examples to get clear reactions.

Start small. Work with small groups of employees and outside audiences to get feedback on the brand modeling. That will give the team a chance to fix glaring errors, add ideas, and refine the examples before moving to larger groups.

If the organization's character requires certainty, or the stakes are simply too high to stumble, move to a larger scale quantitative study. It is simply the only way to bring certainty to ambitious change. Whatever the rigor of the testing, don't mistake feedback for redirection. The process that brought you here guarantees that the overall direction and strategy is sound. The purpose of this research is to ensure that the proposed brand work is communicating what is intended, that the creative and operational changes are doing their job.

For the holdouts and skeptics in the organization, testing is a good way to put their fears to rest. But overall, use this step to refine your approach.

The Washington Center
Internships and Academic Seminars
Internships and Academic Seminars
The Washington Center
The way in. The way ahead.
2010

5. Embed

It is essential to embed the branding work into the organization's culture and processes. The evolution, improvement, and monitoring of the brand experience is not a one-time project. It is an ongoing process that must become part of the fabric of the organization. Making that happen will take effort and time.

For internal audiences, begin with a series of meetings to review the brand work to date. Use the slides and presentations you've developed.

You'll need to publish core materials that present the organization and its brand in a relevant and compelling way. To get everyone on board and inspired, you'll often find that investing in a few superbly written and designed publications can replace dozens of inferior, fragmented materials.

Embedding brand stewardship will take more than good storytelling or materials. It requires training, as well as rewards, for people that protect and build the brand. The goal is to make advancing the new brand part of everyone's job—to rewire the way the organization does things.

Some organizations create specialized brand training programs. Others infuse all employee training with the basics of the brand—who we are and what we do like no other organization.

Often the barrier to a great cohesive brand is that there are no forums or mechanisms to share progress, much less collaborate on the development of programs, products, and communications. The result is dissonance. As you work through the brand building elements of this book, you're actually beginning to create the mechanisms needed to work together across silos.

Make those mechanisms—review of the brand journey, monitoring of key messages, and alignment of behaviors and promises—a permanent part of how the organization gets things done.

TWC needed to tell its story anew to itself, to its alums, to its partners, and to prospective students. The new brand program was launched with core materials, programs, and process changes—on- and off-line. Everything was reconsidered and recast.

BB
B

Identity

Identity is a container of meaning. Meaning that can be trademarked and protected.

What Is Brand Identity?

Brand identity is both a projection and a reflection. A projection that is crafted, monitored, and tuned by "brand stewards," and a reflection of the perceptions and desires of people in and outside of the organization.

Social media has affected that balance—intensifying the ability of others to shape brands. But the force of the crowd has not negated the power of the organization to define its own destiny and brand. The yin and yang of brands has simply become more balanced. That makes for better brands.

In this chapter, we will look at how to craft an effective and enduring brand identity—an identity that communicates the character and purpose of an organization, while remaining compelling and true to the larger world.

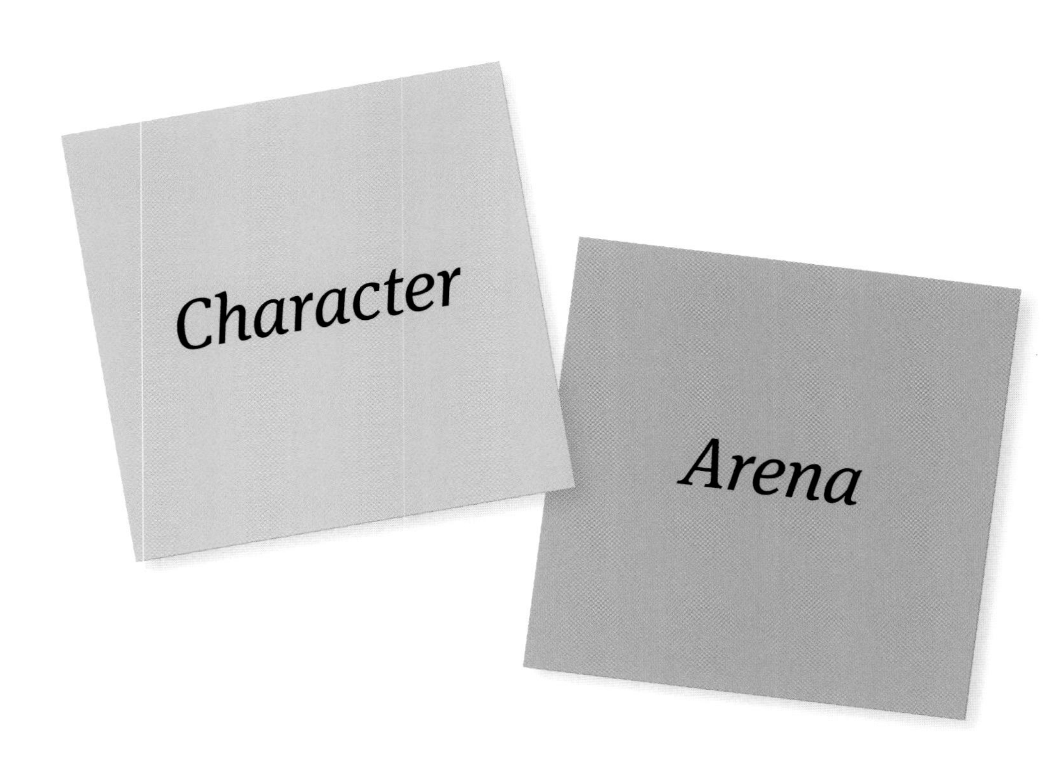

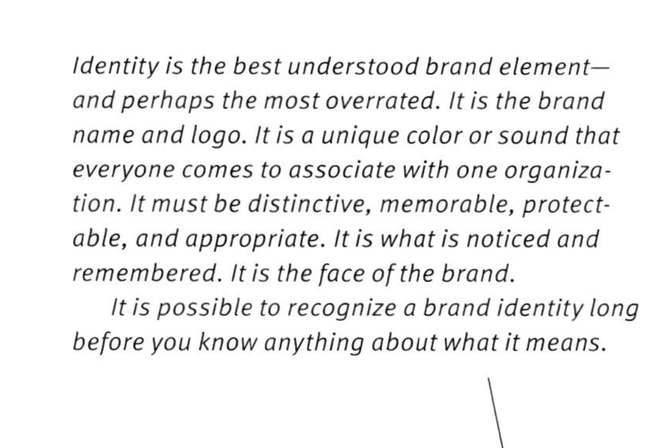

Identity is the best understood brand element—and perhaps the most overrated. It is the brand name and logo. It is a unique color or sound that everyone comes to associate with one organization. It must be distinctive, memorable, protectable, and appropriate. It is what is noticed and remembered. It is the face of the brand.

It is possible to recognize a brand identity long before you know anything about what it means.

Positioning

Experience

Identity

If you've been following the arc of this book, you already know that brand experience is the real world manifestation of the brand. In a sense, it is the content of identity. Brand identity is the container of that content and meaning.

Brands, as you know, were created as a way of marking property—asserting ownership. Trademarks, and later, trademark law, were created to protect the ownership of meaning.

If brand experience is the content of identity, brand identity is its container.

For our purposes, identity includes all of the core elements that form an ownable container for brand meaning.

BRAND IDENTITY

To optimize an existing brand identity, you will need to consider at least five fundamental strategic dimensions.

Equity—the value in existing brand elements. Changing an existing identity is a business and cultural decision. The elements and form may objectively need to evolve or be replaced—but you have to consider the loss of brand recognition and the emotional loss that some will feel if a beloved identity is changed.

Fit—the gap or alignment between what exists and what the brand character and positioning require. This book outlines the development of clear brand definition—a benchmark for the fit of the brand identity. Use that work to assess the gap between what you have and what you need. Align your identity with where you're headed.

Effectiveness—the performance of existing brand elements. In addition to effectiveness of "fit" with the brand definition, consider technical effectiveness. Does the identity attract positive attention? How well is it differentiating the organization from competitors? Does it work well in new media as well as the old? Will it remain legible at small and huge sizes? Do people inside and outside the organization like the identity?

Signal—the magnitude of the "splash" you want to make. Identity is often the most immediate and visible sign of change. Are you trying to quietly evolve? Break with the past? Attract intense attention? Will everything change at once (expensive) or over a long period of time? The intensity of the identity signal can be modulated to fit the strategic parameters.

Cost—The money, time and attention needed to make the new brand program work. For most organizations, the decisions about brand identity change are not actually dictated by costs—just the perceptions of the cost.

Equity
Fit
Effectiveness
Signal
Cost

The reality is that the kind of brand work outlined in this book is almost always tied to substantive strategic change. There's nothing trivial about how a better brand affects the acquisition and retention of customers, talent, investors, and others. The payoff on this kind of effort is substantive, and the larger costs are generally a capital expense that can be depreciated over time.

Identity strategy should be calibrated to balance the sometimes conflicting imperatives of these dimensions.

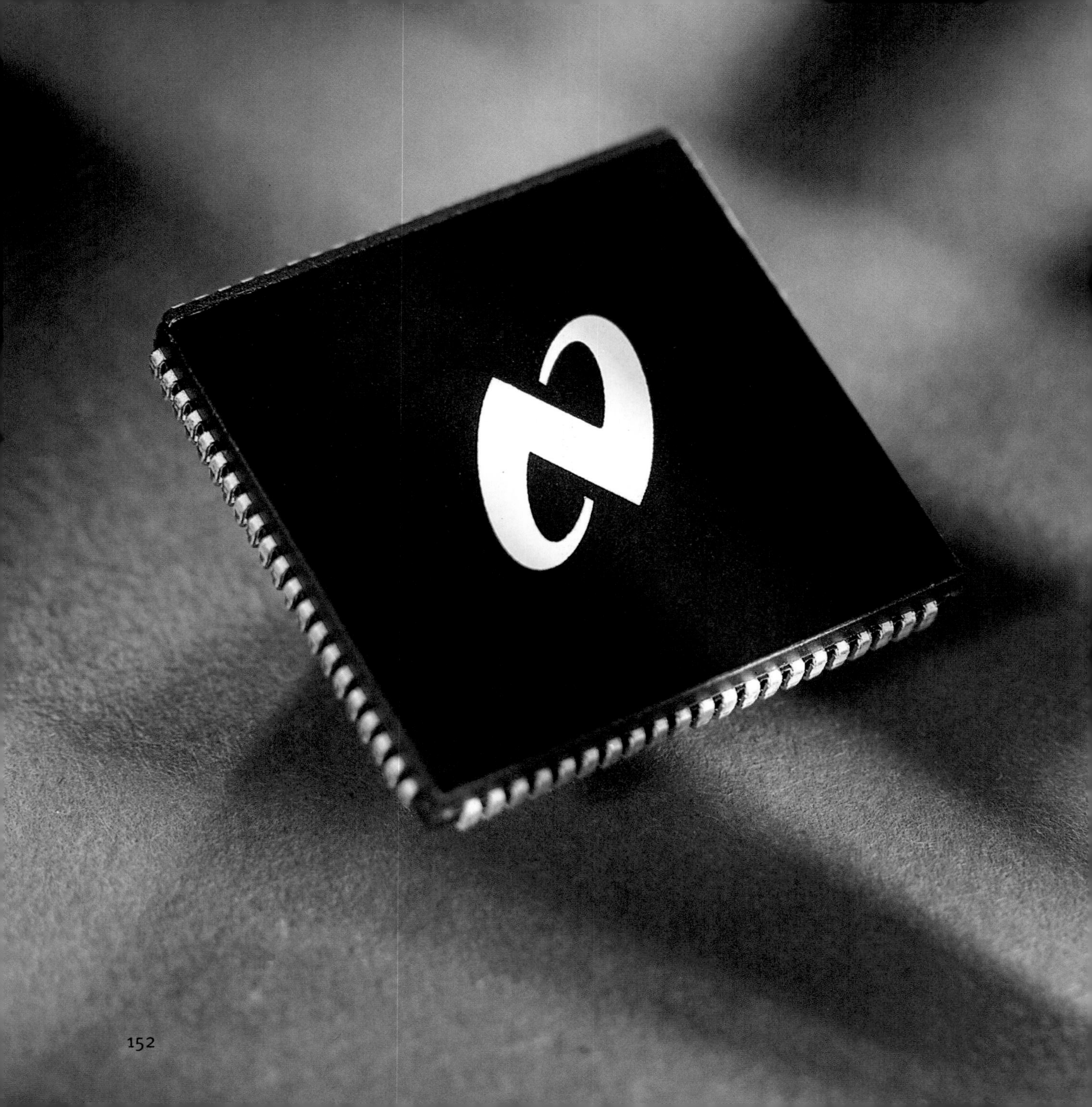

When National Semiconductor (now part of Texas Instruments) recast their brand positioning as the leader in "Moving and Shaping Information," they did not plan to change their logo or other core elements of the corporate identity.

They wanted to retain the equity of the name and "analog waveform" symbol. But when Gil Amelio and his team weighed equity and costs against fit, effectiveness, and signal of change they chose to make a bold move—introducing a new "Worldmark."

The company's leadership also considered shortening the name to "NatSem," but decided that might confuse customers who generally called them "National." By retaining the grand old name and redesigning the symbol to reflect the future, the organization was able to craft a perfectly balanced identity strategy.

National's old symbol and identity program felt dated and irrelevant. The updated identity reflected the new spirit, strategic focus, and success of the company under Gil Amelio.

Brand Architecture

Brand architecture is the relationship of the parts of an organization to the whole—constructed to facilitate access and to position its businesses, brands, products, services, and "ingredients." Brand architecture is a marketing and communications construct that does not have to match an organization's reporting or legal structures.

Sound brand architecture communicates critical information:

- The entity you want the customer to think of as the creator of the products or services
- How tightly your organization's parts are integrated into the whole—one company, a loose confederation, or a portfolio of completely distinct brands
- The parent entity's primary lines of business
- How the parent organizes its products and services
- Ingredient brands that add a specific meaning or enhancement to products

The most common structures used in brand architecture include the following.

Masterbrands. The company is the brand and the brand is the company. Think Bank of America, Harley-Davidson, Barnes & Noble, or McKinsey. While product-lines, service-lines, and individual elements might be branded, the singular masterbrand is dominant.

Endorsed brands. Business and product lines, as well as products and services, may each get their own strong brand. But instead of standing alone, they are endorsed by the parent brand—part of the X family of brands. This structure gives the parts some autonomy, while still providing cohesion. It creates some distance between the parent and other brands, but gives them the benefit of the parent's goodwill.

House of brands. Some parent companies are overseers, letting their brands stand as individual entities. From the market's point of view, each brand looks like a parent. This structure might be used by a private equity company that owns diverse businesses or a consumer goods conglomerate that owns brands like Ben & Jerry's.

Doing so enables a single parent to market disparate products and services, even multiple brands that compete in the same arena. For example, Unilever can market both AXE and Dove—brands that are incompatible from a character and positioning perspective—because few know of their shared parent.

Ingredient brands. Brands like INVISTA's LYCRA® act as ingredients in products and services. This brand structure is very flexible, even allowing other companies to use the brand in combination with their own.

Hybrids. Many organizations use hybrid brand architectures. Most of their businesses are sheltered under a single masterbrand umbrella, while some are endorsed, stand alone, or act as ingredients.

Study the brand attribute maps that you developed in the positioning analysis. They show how closely the parts can be related in meaning for key audiences. That's a good start for defining a working structure. But you'll need to consider other factors.

You should weigh risk as a factor in designing a brand architecture. Unproven businesses might be best launched as endorsed brands. Also, if you plan to spin-off or sell a business, you should grow it as an endorsed or stand-alone brand. This will make it easy to prune off without sacrificing its market recognition.

How do the parts of the brand fit together? What is the optimal hierarchy and visibility of the elements? Should you build a single large brand structure or a number of smaller ones?

It's not difficult to research brand architecture. Explore the corporate as well as marketing websites of brands in your arena and beyond. You'll be able to see how each organization is structuring its offer.

The corporate websites will reveal the hidden structure of a house of brands (like Unilever.) And the consumer-facing sites are designed to showcase the brand(s) in exactly the way they'd like them to be seen by the outside world.

Ingredient brands, such as LYCRA® and Dolby®, will be integrated into many websites—the parent corporate site, as well as the product promotion sites of customers that use the equity of an ingredient brand to enhance their own.

Some organizations opt for a hybrid strategy where the majority of the company is masterbranded, but some parts are allowed to project their own distinct brand.

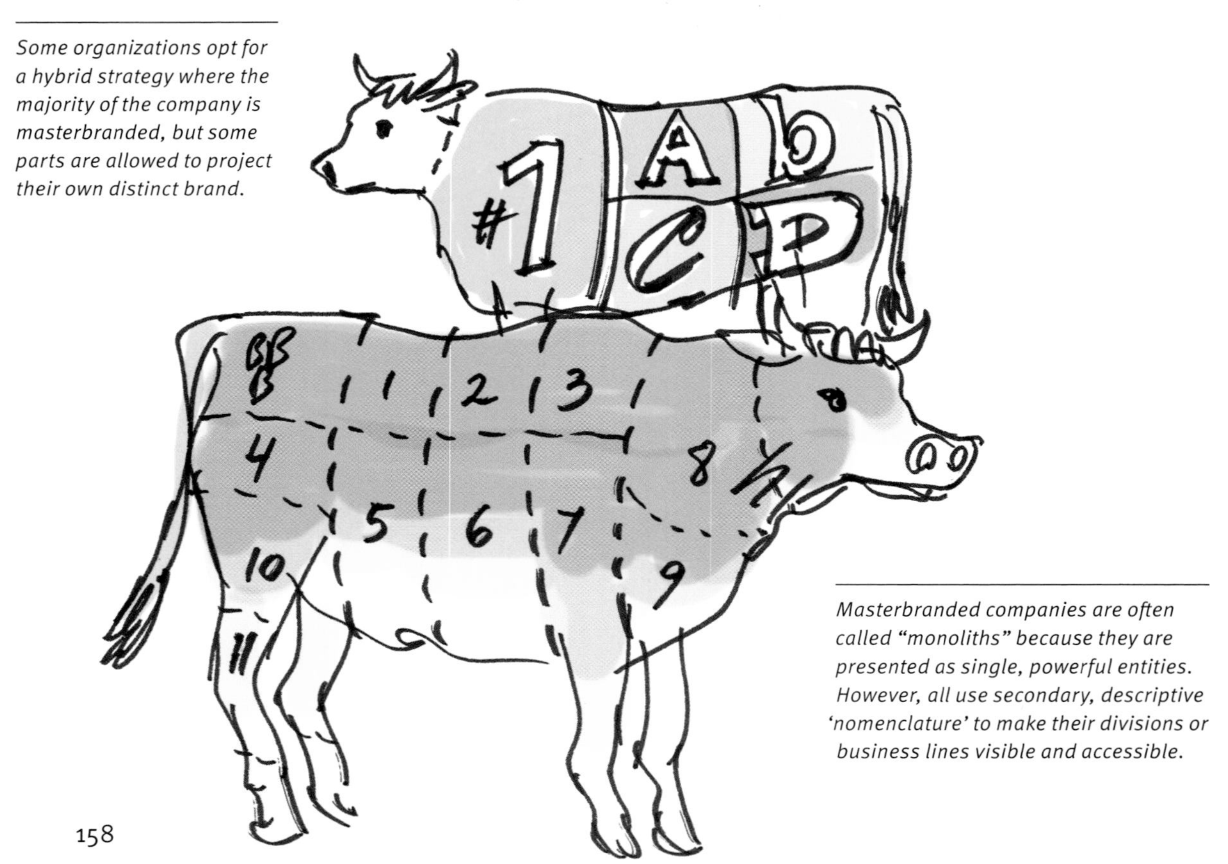

Masterbranded companies are often called "monoliths" because they are presented as single, powerful entities. However, all use secondary, descriptive 'nomenclature' to make their divisions or business lines visible and accessible.

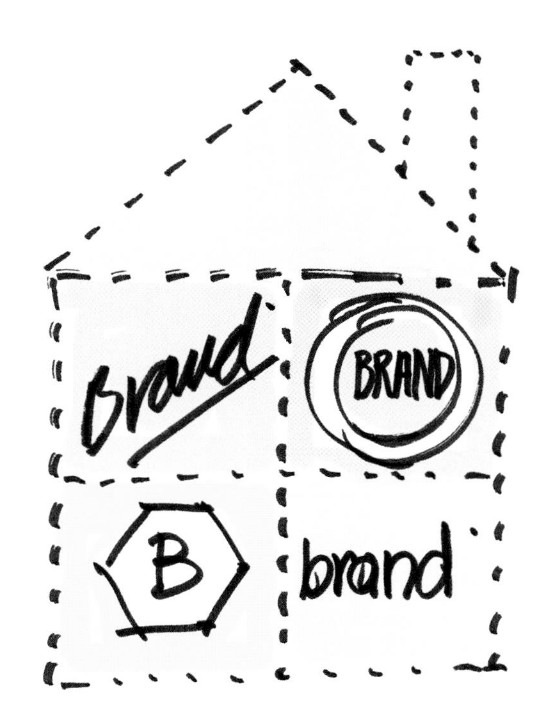

A house of brands is defined by the brands it holds. This strategy allows an organization to field multiple brands—even competitive brands—each with its own character, identity, and strategic positioning.

Ingredient brands are designed to coexist with other brands while adding meaning and value.

Look and Feel

No great discovery was ever made without a bold guess —Isaac Newton

If you never did, you should. These things are fun and fun is good. —Dr. Seuss

Brand ideas must be translated into creative expression. Much of the work of redesigning, rewriting, re-architecting, and rejuvenating an organization's identity elements (like logos), communications, marketing, spaces, and behavior will be done with specialists. But everyone in the organization should understand the importance of aligning expression with the ideas that define the brand.

One of the best ways to train people to connect ideas and expression is to let them work through the process.

Create a broad array of look and feel flashcards: I call them "VisionCards." Select phrases that imply behavior or communicate character. Select images that depict a broad range of situations, architecture, typefaces, metaphors, and interactions. Include colors from primary to pastel. Your stack of VisionCards can be very large and range from the sublime to cliché.

Start the workshop with a review of the new brand strategy and definitions. Put those definitions on the wall for everyone to reference as they work.

Then break the participants into teams. Give each a full set of VisionCards, one sheet of letter-sized paper, and a gluestick.

Ask the groups to decide if each image fits the arena, character, and brand positioning. Yes or no? Set the clock to count down 30 minutes. They will need to work fast!

Each group should winnow down the VisionCards to only the ones that best communicate the ideas that define the organization's brand—no more than can fit on that single sheet of paper. Once they're sure—and before the time is up—they should paste the images down.

Shoot a digital image of each and project the VisionCard collages onto a large screen. Talk about why they chose those specific images. Discuss the similarities and differences across the groups.

This kind of discussion will help people understand that selecting visual elements, choosing words, guiding interactions with customers, and even designing offices should not be discrete, random acts. Everything must use the brand as a benchmark.

This workshop is also useful for the pros who will actually develop the final look and feel of the brand. It lets them see how the people of the organization, across divisions and geographies, select and react to potential identity elements.

Choosing images, colors, concepts, and language that "fit" the brand character and positioning is an effective way to build an understanding—even with non-designers—of the process of turning ideas into expression.

Names

Names are an elemental part of identity. Even organizations that use only a symbol on their communications do so knowing that their name, although unwritten, is heard in the mind of viewers.

To evaluate the effectiveness of an existing name or develop a new name you'll have to decide what's most important for the name to accomplish. Is it to describe what you do? Or is it more important for the name suggest an idea derived from the brand positioning? Do you want to arbitrarily redefine, then own anew, the meaning of an existing word? Or do you want to invent a fanciful new word or sound that's yours alone?

The terms generic, descriptive, suggestive, arbitrary, and fanciful are terms of art from trademark law. The listing at right is sorted from least protectable to most; from self-explanatory to baffling (without explanation and serious marketing support).

You can't trademark a purely generic name. Shoe Inc. couldn't be registered today. (That is, unless Shoe Inc. was the name of a muffin store—it would then be classified as an arbitrary name.)

Creating names is a winnowing process. You'll need to create dozens, sometimes hundreds of possibilities. The reason is that most will already be taken—used by an organization in the same industry category (or classification). Spelling differences don't matter; it is the sound that determines the conflict.

We won't get into trademark law here, but use this simple rule of thumb—if the name will cause confusion with a competitor's, and they have used it first, you cannot use that name.

You'll also want to eliminate possible names if you can't register the Internet address. That's also getting more and more difficult. Again, one advantage of a fanciful name is that when you invent words you've got a better chance of getting the URL.

You may also find that it is hard to evaluate names. Many people dislike any new name when they first hear it. Use the name in a sentence. Show it in use on a business card or sign mock-up. Live with it a while.

Trademarked names can be descriptive, suggestive, arbitrary, or fanciful—like "BabyOne," "Mischievous," "Acorn," and "Booboo."

Generic

Purely generic terms cannot be trademarked and should not be used for organization or company names.

Descriptive

Descriptive names like *U.S. Steel* are purely descriptive—nearly generic.

Suggestive

Names that suggest an idea, like *Fast Company*, are more differentiating than descriptive names. They add a layer of concept and personality.

Arbitrary

Arbitrary names, like *Apple*, make for very strong trademarks, but you'll have to teach people to associate the name with something entirely different than its accepted meaning. Also, the same name can be used as a trademark in a different classification of goods and services, e.g., *Apple* records.

Fanciful

Fanciful names, like *Kodak*, are invented. Which makes them the strongest trademarks. You invent it, use it, and trademark it. No one else can use it.

Stronger trademark but requires explanation

Weaker trademark but is self-explanatory

The stronger the idea of the name, the easier it is to like. I remember disliking Novartis when it was born. But it has become a favorite over time, in part because it was inspired by the idea of "New arts in the science of life." Nova, new. Artis, arts. Another suggestive/fanciful name with a great back-story is "INVISTA"—built from the combined ideas of "innovative" and "vista."

Naming and trademark law are specialized professions. Your job is to keep that work focused on the brand ideas you've defined. Insist on getting this right.

Logos

Logos are the stars of identity. Content, color, imagery, typography, form, and other elements often have a more profound effect on the unconscious recognition of a brand—but what people will think of, remember, is the logo.

For our purposes a logo is any name, symbol, or combination that has been graphically designed to distinguish the goods or services of one source from another. (That's a definition derived from U.S. trademark law.)

The terms commonly used for different forms of logos (or logotypes) varies. Generally, **wordmarks** are purely typographic, but may fully integrate a graphic element into the name. **Signatures** are simply wordmarks that have an accompanying symbol. And some brands have such recognizable **symbols** that they begin to use them without an accompanying wordmark. Nike is a classic example, but Starbucks has also begun to use its "Siren" symbol as a standalone logo after 40 years of being used in combination with the name.

New or updated logo development should be done in parallel with the experience modeling discussed in the preceeding chapter. As the experience is evolved, an existing logo may begin to look dated or out-of-place. They need to work hand-in-glove.

Pulpbranding.com has two issues devoted to "LogoDoc," an unsung design hero who helps rescue logos in danger of becoming cliché or dated.

What comes first, the experience or the identity?

1. Evaluate

Creating or recasting a brand identity is a significant undertaking. Organizations often jump too quickly from brand definition to identity development.

If you've followed the process outlined in this book, you have modeled the optimal brand experience of key audiences, which gives you a distinct advantage. Instead of evaluating brand identity elements—like names, logos, and look and feel—purely in abstract terms, you have a real-world framework in which to evaluate your ideas.

The goal of this step is to consider the strategic fit of an identity, as well as how it might actually look, feel, sound, and behave in the marketplace. Think of it as a simulation of the future.

This approach creates a bit of the "chicken or egg" dilemma. You will have initially modeled the experience without knowing the final form and function of the brand identity. As the final identity emerges, it will affect the experience.

For example, you may decide to change the organization name to better reflect its character. A more evocative name may take some of the burden off of content or imagery to convey character. Or, a new logo may use a distinctive form or color that needs to be echoed and amplified over the course of a customer's journey.

Just work back and forth between experience modeling and identity development. Let that cycle of refining the experience/identity continue until they are in perfect harmony. Like many steps in this book, moving forward, then back, then forward again is a natural and valuable part of getting to the right solution.

The work plan for identity development is straightforward. Start by evaluating the core identity elements. Explore how they might be improved, or if appropriate, recast. Remodel the experience. Repeat until right. Then test, refine, and codify the final identity solution.

IDENTITY

*work*PLAN

1. Evaluate

2. (re)Model

3. Test

4. Codify

Strategy
Look & feel
Name
Logo

Many organizations go into the process of refining their brand with a strong sense of what they will, or will not change.

That bias isn't necessarily bad. In general, it is prudent to have a bias toward retaining past equity. Don't throw away a recognizable identity unless it no longer gives you sufficient competitive advantage.

In some instances, an identity is too tainted to survive. A recent example is GMAC (General Motors Acceptance Corporation.) The global financial meltdown made its name a liability, so they decided they needed to replace it (with Ally) and try to make a fresh start.

Overall, however, your core identity team should not accept any bias at face value. The Tyco brand was tainted by a leadership scandal, but they chose to fix the leadership issue, put in safeguards, and relaunch the brand. Your responsibility is to weigh the meaning and value of core identity elements to reach effective and efficient solutions.

What exactly are you evaluating?

First, identity strategy. It is not the same as brand strategy. Brand strategy is the benchmark for meaning. Identity strategy is a coherent approach and plan to bringing the brand strategy to life in the marketplace.

Second, look and feel. This is the written voice, color, typography, style, sound, imagery, smell, and texture of the brand; everything and anything that gives it shape and substance.

Third, the brand name. To name something is literally to identify it.

Fourth, the logo. Often a combination of name and symbol, the logo is the most elemental container of brand meaning.

IDENTITY

*work*PLAN

1. Evaluate
2. (re)Model
3. Test
4. Codify

1994 Annual Report

National Semiconductor

Technologies for
Moving and Shaping Information

2. Re(Model)

Using the identity evaluation as a basis, go back and remodel the brand experience. Incorporate potential changes to the name, logo, color, language, imagery, and other elements.

Begin to expand and enrich the brand modeling. The work you do now has to build on what's been done before. Consider involving more people, including outside creative resources like your ad, public relations, and web agencies in the process. This is your chance to ensure that the identity you've created has the depth to work in the long term.

You can also begin to ask functional groups, like legal, facilities, investor relations, human resources, and others to weigh in. Is the emerging brand identity and experience understandable, relevant, and compelling?

IDENTITY

*work*PLAN

1. Evaluate

2. (re)Model

3. Test

4. Codify

"If I want something real high performance, I don't even open their catalog."

"I had no idea!"

3. Test

The remodeling process provides an organization with the ideal research stimuli to test the clarity, credibility, distinctiveness, and potential effect of the brand experience and identity.

By letting key audiences react to realistic sets of materials and messages, you will get genuine reactions. Piecemeal research on names, symbols, and other elements can be useful along the way, but this kind of stimuli is needed to make sure the whole, not just the pieces, are accomplishing your goals.

Testing should not be limited to customers, investors, donors, and other kinds of external audiences. Employees and partners should be included. If your own people and channels don't understand or aren't inspired by the change, why should outsiders care?

Still, it's best to start with outside testing and then share the results internally. Most insiders won't fully accept any change unless they're sure it will be a success with outside audiences.

Start with qualitative research—perhaps focus groups—to get a feel for how your audiences might react. Learn and refine. Then consider quantitative research to prove that you will positively move the marketplace.

Document the focus groups. There's nothing like hearing a positive reaction from the mouth of a valued customer to build excitement and support for ambitious change.

After being presented with the new brand and identity strategy, this group went from an uninformed view of National Semiconductor to genuine, strong, (and surprised) interest in their products...

National addressed the issues and fears of the organization head-on. That honesty helped make the introduction of the new brand positioning and identity an unqualified success.

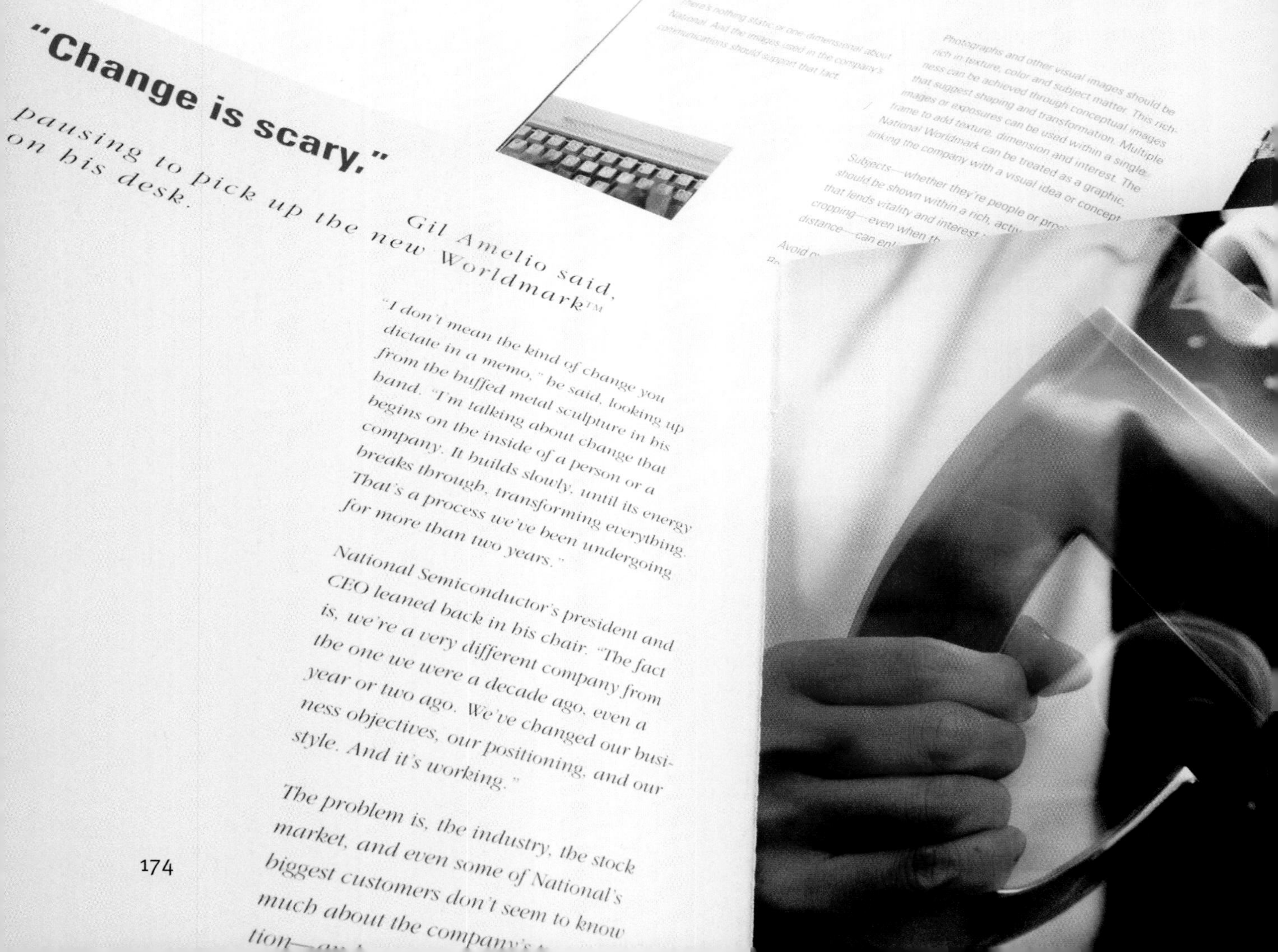

"Change is scary,"

Gil Amelio said, pausing to pick up the new Worldmark™ on his desk.

"I don't mean the kind of change you dictate in a memo," he said, looking up from the buffed metal sculpture in his hand. "I'm talking about change that begins on the inside of a person or a company. It builds slowly, until its energy breaks through, transforming everything. That's a process we've been undergoing for more than two years."

National Semiconductor's president and CEO leaned back in his chair. "The fact is, we're a very different company from the one we were a decade ago, even a year or two ago. We've changed our business objectives, our positioning, and our style. And it's working."

The problem is, the industry, the stock market, and even some of National's biggest customers don't seem to know much about the company's

Imaging National

There's nothing static or one-dimensional about National. And the images used in the company's communications should support that fact.

Photographs and other visual images should be rich in texture, color and subject matter. This richness can be achieved through conceptual images that suggest shaping and transformation. Multiple images or exposures can be used within a single frame to add texture, dimension and interest. The National Worldmark can be treated as a graphic, linking the company with a visual idea or concept.

4. Codify

Efforts to codify brand identity programs and communicate them across an organization usually focus on logo, color, and typographic and other technical specifications. But this isn't enough to ensure success.

Tell the whole story of the creation or evolution of the brand. Spend as much time explaining the journey as the destination. While identity standards, rules, and regulations are for the pros, the ideas and principles are for everyone.

Sometimes it's best to produce smaller, targeted documents (on- and off-line) for specific users. They make it far easier to speak in understandable terms and give people a clear sense of their role in protecting and advancing the brand and brand identity.

1. Evaluate

2. (re)Model

3. Test

4. Codify

EENY, MEENY, MINY, MOE
CATCH A TIGER BY THE TOE
IF HE HOLLERS LET HIM GO
EENY, MEENY,
MINY,
MOE!

Help!

You Can't Do This Alone

The intent of this book is to give you a sense of the arc of a significant brand development program—the path to a better brand. While the journey may still be a bit blurry, you now have a map to think ahead and identify areas where you'll need help. You can't do this alone, so you'll need to decide who to bring into the process.

Some of the people with the right skills may be in-house. Many organizations have research and trademark expertise, others a talented group of designers. But few have all of the necessary specialized skills in research, business strategy, brand positioning, identity development, and trademark protection—as well as expertise in training and implementation.

So how do you find outside help?

The largest brand consulting firms are easy to find. Just Google "top 10 branding firms." In the corporate branding arena, they're all owned by giant public companies like IPG, WPP, and Omnicom. For a multinational client that's looking for global reach in implementation and ongoing communications development, the larger firms may be a good choice. Their unique advantages are in "asset" and "offer" attributes.

Medium and small brand consulting firms are fundamentally different. They are often independent, private firms. They pride (and position) themselves on process, skills, and mission attributes.

You'll learn about smaller firms through word-of-mouth, organizations like the Design Management Institute and the AIGA, and by hunting down the firms behind brand programs you admire. Most smaller firms don't have the resources to market their prowess on a large scale. (Some write books to become better known.)

So how do you choose? You move through the gates of choice.

All reasonable efforts have been made to insure the accuracy of the content of this book, which seeks to offer guidance. However, the suggestions and advice contained in this text are not meant to be replace legal, trademark and strategic counsel.

THERE ARE SO MANY POSSIBILITIES...
GLOBAL GIANT
X-TREME
MAN AND A DOG
NEURO DESIGN
SAGE
SHINY NEW
E=MC2

Arena. If you want a better brand for a new line of candy bars, consider a branding firm that specializes in FMCG (fast moving consumer goods). If you want to brand the company that makes candy bars and more, compile a long-list of prospective corporate branding consultancies.

Positioning. Unless you require a firm that owns a global network, scale won't be the most important driver of choice. Approach, skills, and/or mission attributes will be the decisive factors.

Both large and small firms can be "approach"-driven. As the industry has matured, the approaches used have become relatively similar—although often touted as unique. The real differences will be more in the emphasis placed on parts of the process.

Some firms believe in rigorous research, others in creative leaps. There are firms that are design-led and others that are strategy-led. Others will strive for a balance of strategic thinking and creativity.

Character. As you now know, character is the most important factor in final choice. You need to know with whom you will be working. The only way to be sure is to meet the people who would work on your project—not the firm's principals or the business development staff that sells programs.

Gauge the experience, drive, and talent of the team you'd be working with. Ask them to talk in-depth about the projects they've led. Make sure you like and trust them.

Experience. Talk with the team's past clients about what happened along the way, not just the results. That's the best way to get a sense of what it will really be like to work with them. Again, you want references for the people you will work with, not just the firm.

1. *Meet face-to-face with prospective firms.*
2. *Insist on a meeting with the working team, not just super-salespeople.*
3. *Review a few case studies, in depth with the team, not just "beauty-shots".*
4. *Ask for and talk with references.*
5. *Make sure the firm really wants your business!*

These are some of the attributes that are part of the brand consulting arena. Which are most important to your choice? Which are just table-stakes?

Many years in business
Excellent track record
Locations across the world
Satisfied clients (past/present)
Works with leading companies
Superb testimonials
Award winning
Sound technical infrastructure
Public company
Private company
Certifications
No client conflicts
Long-tenured staff/leadership
Client retention
Redundancy
Great portfolio
Network of suppliers
Network of distributors
Low-cost structure
World-class facilities
Builds enduring brands
Retains top talent
Is recognized as a leader

Assets

What we own and control

End-to-end brand development
Brand research
Brand audit
Brand strategy
Brand expression
Brand identity
Brand systems
Brand launch
Brand implementation
Brand communications
Brand social media
Brand marketing
Brand management
Brand valuation
Brand—etc.
Good value
Cheap
Premium

Offer

Our products and services

Well-managed
Treats you like a partner
Able to work with senior leaders
Puts the client first
Transparent business practices
Fairly resolves issues
Culturally sensitive
Senior people do the project work
Superb client management skills
Makes client partners successful
Cogent program roadmaps
Clear cost structure
Monitors success metrics
Tight quality controls
Encourages experimentation
Constantly evolving
Straightforward and simple
Ability to quickly scale operations
Collaborative
Shares risks/rewards
Well defined team structures
Provides alternatives
Modeling/prototyping
No surprises on scope/costs
Superb internal controls
Applies a diverse array of talent
Always delivers
Customizes approach to fit goals
Is innovative
Candid

Approach

How we do things

Industry expertise
Great credentials
Experienced, top-level people
Cross-disciplined
Diverse
Specialized
Renowned staff
Relate well to leadership
Able to engage the entire organization
Able to unify organizations
Good teachers
Great leaders
Fast learners
Proven/certified/licensed
Rare talent
Unique
Good under pressure
Detail-oriented
Strong problem-solving skills
Cultural, linguistic skills
Superior insight and creativity
Passionate about branding
World-class designers
World-class strategists
World-class researchers
World-class project managers
World-class new media staff
World-class—etc.

Skills

The skills we apply

"Green"
Social agenda...
Triple bottom line...

Mission

The ideals that drive us

While small firms have always existed to develop local and small-scale corporate identity and branding programs (or elements of larger programs), it is only in the last decade that David can and does compete with Goliath.

Today, it is the quality of expertise, thinking, and creative talent—not scale—that are the most valued factors in the choice of brand consultants. Approach and skills are the key drivers of choice.

SIZE IS NO LONGER SUCH A "BIG" ADVANTAGE.

N

Afterword

By Debbie Millman

Contemporary culture is now nearly entirely composed of brands. Everything we eat, wear, share and sell—even our most basic commodities like water and salt—are brands. Experiences are brands. People are brands. Our role models are people; therefore our role models are brands. Brands are so persuasive in their personal, social, sexual, political, economic, aesthetic, psychological, and ethical consequences that they impact every single aspect of our reality. Any knowledge of culture now is impossible without an understanding of the implications of "brand." We have entered a day and age where brand is an extension of human affect and behavior.

As a result, the financial, functional and emotional importance of brands and their use as a marketing tool has highlighted the need for rigorous academic and business investigation. The impact of "branding" as a tool to guide innovation and change are more evident than at any other time in our history, and there is no evidence of this diminishing anytime soon. Branding is now inextricably linked to the way in which society, culture, the environment, and business interact and communicate.

Scott Lerman's brilliant new book provides a robust examination of how, why, and when branding is necessary and how to create or redesign brands in a vibrant, compelling, authentic, and compelling way. It is a must-read for anyone and everyone who is interested in why branding matters more than ever before.

More

There is so much more to talk about, learn, and share—but I vowed to keep this guide to 100 spreads of core content. I hope these pages have given you an actionable sense of how to develop a substantive brand program. I know there will be unanswered questions along the way, so here are some sources to tap when you are stuck or want to go deeper.

ikonica
A Field Guide to Canada's Brandscape
Jeannette Hanna // Alan Middleton
Olins
Wally Olins: The Brand Handbook
Brand
book
Thames & Hudson

BRAND BIBLE
ROCKPORT
EDITED BY DEBBIE MILLMAN
THE COMPLETE GUIDE TO BUILDING, DESIGNING, AND SUSTAINING BRANDS
THE ONE TO ONE FUTURE
Building Relationships One Customer at a Time
CURRENCY DOUBLEDAY
"Book of the Year" —Tom Peters
"Peters was wrong. This is not the book of the year. It's not even the book of the decade. It's one of the two or three most important business books ever written." —GEORGE GENDRON Inc. magazine
DON PEPPERS and MARTHA ROGERS, PH.D.
INCLUDING AN ALL-NEW USER'S GUIDE

www.aiga.org

www.branding.sva.edu

www.designobserver.com

www.dmi.org

www.identityworks.com/forum

www.ikonographic.com

www.lucidbrands.com

www.pulpbranding.com

www.ted.com

www.underconsideration.com

Thanks!

I'd like to thank a few of the many people and organizations that have helped me along the way.

Carol, Menchu, and Van for sharing their thoughts in the "Champions" section.

Will Ayres for contributing so many great drawings to illuminate the ideas in this book.

Juan Carlos Fernández Espinosa and Jeannette Hanna for their valued perspectives.

The many companies mentioned in this book—their presence here is not an endorsement of any kind and their trademarks, shown for educational purposes only, remain their undisputed property.

Susan Keiser, my partner at Lucid Brands (and beyond), for her unwavering support and incisive thinking.

Debbie Millman, the co-founder of SVA's MPS Branding program that so kindly let me become a part of educating the next generation of "brand masters."

Chermayeff & Geismar, Siegel+Gale, and Enterprise IG, firms where I learned the business and craft of branding and identity from mentors and colleagues that included Tom Geismar, Steff Geissbuhler, Alan Siegel, Don Ervin, Anne Breaznell, Ron Manzke, Ken Cooke, Rolf Wulfsberg, Robert Saporito, and many, many others.

Clients who have taught me more than I've taught them—too many to list here!

A Brief Bio

Scott Lerman has built his career by helping companies navigate critical moments in the creation, transition, and extension of their brands. His broad and deep expertise in integrated brand consulting, research, corporate identity, naming, design, and implementation comes from nearly three decades as a leader and practitioner.

In 2005, Scott founded Lucid Brands, a brand consultancy dedicated to the development of world-class brands. Before founding Lucid Brands, Scott led two leading brand consultancies. During his 17 years at Siegel+Gale he held a range of senior positions, including President. In 2001, he was named President and CEO of Enterprise IG, Americas (now The Brand Union). He started his career in brand identity with a humble stint as a paste-up artist at the legendary firm, Chermayeff & Geismar.

Over the years, Scott has led defining brand engagements with 3M, American Express, Bayer, Caterpillar, DuPont, Engelhard, First Data, Grand Brands, Harley-Davidson, INVISTA, JCPenney, Kodak, Lycos, The Metropolitan Transportation Authority (MTA), National Semiconductor, Owens-Illinois, PNC Bank, Readers Digest, SWIFT, Towers Perrin, The U.S. Mint, VOIS, The Washington Center, Xerox, Yola, Zachry and dozens of other organizations around the world. He is currently seeking a client with a corporate name that starts with "Q".

Scott is on the founding faculty of the School of Visual Arts Masters in Branding program. He has explored the issues shaping businesses and brands in *The Design Management Review*, *The Wall Street Journal*, *The New York Times*, *Identity, Revolution*, and other publications. He is on the advisory council of The Design Management Institute and served on the founding board of the AIGA's branding chapter. Scott has lectured at Columbia University, Thunderbird School of Global Management, J.P. Morgan, Apple, AMA, and many other outstanding organizations.

To learn more, go to www.lucidbrands.com

Permissions

3M and Post-It® are registered trademarks owned by 3M Company and used under permission.

American Red Cross logo, The American Red Cross logo is a registered trademark of the American Red Cross.

Bayer taglines, Bayer Corporation © 1998

Brand Bible, book cover image, © Debbie Millman 2012

Brand Handbook, The, book cover image, Saffron Brand Consultants, LTD © 2008

BrightPoint film keyframe "storyboard", Brightpoint Identity and Visual System Developed by BrandTaxi LLC. Brightpoint, Inc. © 2012

Caterpillar trademark and liscensed articles, ® Caterpillar Inc.

Container Store logo and The Container Store logo in a chart, 2013 © The Container Store, Inc.

DuPont oval logo is a trademark of Dupont ® or its affiliates.

FedEx website image used with permission. FedEx® is a registered trademark of Federal Express Corporation.

Gee interview and likeness used with permission of Carol Gee.

Home Depot, The and the Home Depot ® logo are trademarks of Homer TLC, Inc. used under license.

Iknonica book cover image, Jeannette Hanna © 2008

INVISTA mark and corresponding logo used with permission of INVISTA™.

L'EGGS packaging image used with permission of Hanesbrands Inc. L'EGGS ® logo is a registered trademark of Hanesbrands Inc.

Mendiola-Fernández interview and likeness used with permission from Carmenchu Mendiola-Fernández.

Metropolitan Transportation Authority (MTA) logo and related images used with permission of MTA. All images (archival MTA map; image of an MTA train featuring an archival logo; image of an MTA subway car; image of an MTA bus featuring an archival logo; image of an MTA Bridges & Tunnels vehicle featuring an archival logo; and image of a subway station featuring an archival NYCTA logo) © Metropolitan Transportation Authority. Used with Permission. Trademarked material (MTA logo; MTA blue MetroCard; MTA subway token; and New York City Transit Authority logo) ® Metropolitan Transportation Authority. Used with Permission. All editorial materials in the book regarding the MTA are those of the author and not of MTA.

McKinsey & Company logo and McKinsey & Company logo in a chart, © McKinsey & Company.

Mr. Peanut ™ image used with permission of Kraft Foods Brands LLC.

National Semiconductor logo and photos courtesy of Texas Instruments © 2013

One to One Future, The, book cover image, Don Peppers and Martha Rogers, Phd © 1993

OXO potato peeler photo used with permission of OXO. OXO® and GoodGrips® are registered trademarks of Helen of Troy, Limited.

Perry interview and likeness used with permission from Van Perry.

TUI Marine communications audit materials used with permission from TUI Marine.

Washington Center logo and images used with permission from The Washington Center for Internships and Academic Seminars © 2013.

Washington Center (depictions of the The Washington Center publications using Jeff Newton photos), Jeff Newton Studio LLC © 2013

All other illustrations in the book were created by Will Ayres. Will Ayres © 2013.

Index

More Great Titles from HOW Books

Archetypes in Branding

By Margaret Pott Hartwell & Joshua C. Chen

Archetypes in Branding: A Toolkit for Creatives and Strategists gives you an effective and incredibly practical tool for branding and marketing. Using a highly participatory approach to branding strategies, combined with sixty beautiful (and incredibly useful) brand archetype cards, this kit offers you a creative and intuitive tool for charting a course for your brand.

Build Your Own Brand

By Robin Landa

Whether your goal is to land a new design project or launch your own business, this personal branding guide can help put you on the path to success. *Build Your Own Brand* will help you differentiate yourself, create your own brand identity and craft a personal branding statement. You'll find helpful advice, interviews and prompts from esteemed psychologists, creative directors, brand strategists, designers, artists and experts from a variety of disciplines.

Special Offer From HOW Books!

You can get **15%** off your entire order at **MyDesignShop.com!** All you have to do is go to **www.howdesign.com/howbooks-offer** and sign up for our free e-newsletter on graphic design. You'll also get a free digital download of HOW magazine.

For more news, tips and articles, follow us at **Twitter.com/HOWbrand**

For behind-the-scenes information and special offers, become a fan at **Facebook.com/HOWmagazine**

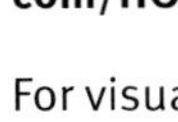

For visual inspiration, follow us at **Pinterest.com/HOWbrand**

Find these books and many others at MyDesignShop.com or your local bookstore.